I joined while having a crisis with Amazon KDP... The Alliance is a beacon of light. I recommend that all indie authors join...

Susan Marshall

The Alliance is about standing together.

Joanna Penn

It's the good stuff, all on one place.

Richard Wright

"ALLi has helped me in myriad ways: discounts on services, vetting providers, charting a course to sales success. But more than anything it's a community of friendly, knowledgeable, helpful people."

Beth Duke

See hundreds more testimonials at:
AllianceIndependentAuthors.org/testimonials

INDIE AUTHOR MAGAZINE

LAUNCH STRATEGIES

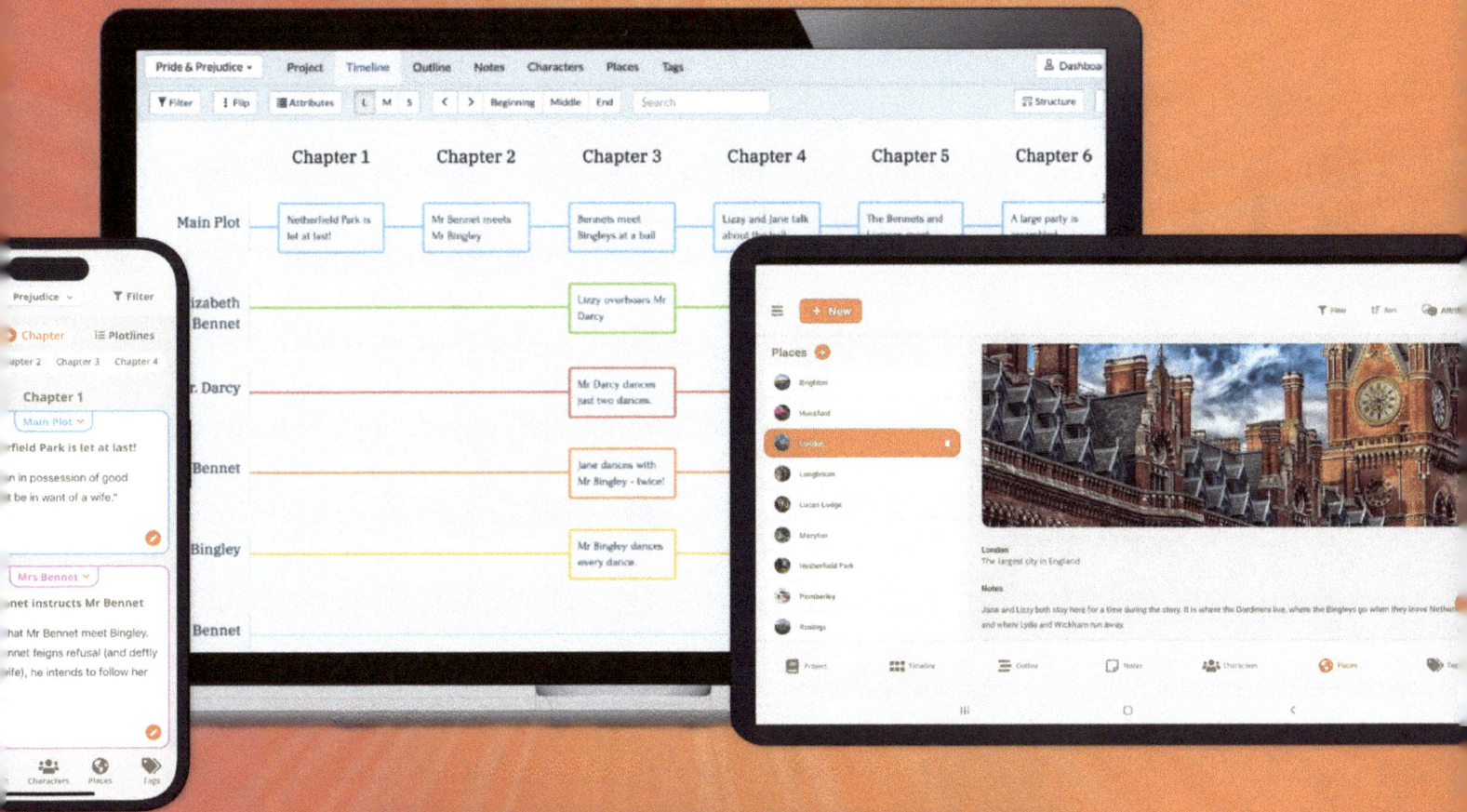

Authorpreneurs in Action

"I love Lulu! They've been a fantastic distributor of my paperbacks and an excellent partner as I dive into direct sales. They integrate so smoothly with my personal Shopify store, and their customer support has been top notch."

Katie Cross, katiecrossbooks.com

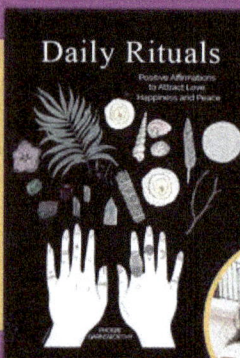

"Having my own store has given me the freedom to look at my creativity as a profitable business and lifelong career."

Phoebe Garnsworthy, phoebegarnsworthy.com

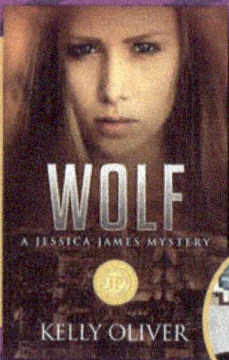

"Lulu has a super handy integration with Shopify. Lulu makes it so easy to sell paperbacks directly to readers."

Kelly Oliver, kellyoliverbooks.com

"My experience with Lulu Direct has been more convenient and simple than I anticipated or thought possible. I simply publish, take a step back and allow the well-oiled machine to run itself. Most grateful!"

Molly McGivern, theactorsalmanac.com

lulu *direct*

Sell Smarter, Not Harder.

Sell Books from Your Website Using Lulu Direct

Keep 100% of your profit

Retain customer data

Integrate with Shopify, WooCommerce, Zapier, & Custom API

Get paid quickly

FREE — No monthly fees

Fully automated white-label fulfillment

Global print network

B Corp Certified

Dropshipping Multiple Orders for a New Book Launch or Crowdfunding Campaign? Use the Lulu Order Import Tool!

We make dropshipping multiple orders at once easier than ever!

- ✓ Upload your book on Lulu for free
- ✓ Use the Order Import Tool to upload a file with your customer's order and shipping information
- ✓ We'll professionally print the orders and drop ship each one to your fans around the world

Get exclusive Publishing & Marketing tips to help you create and sell your books more effectively!

INDIE
AUTHOR MAGAZINE

EDITORIAL

Publisher | Chelle Honiker

Editor in Chief | Nicole Schroeder

Creative Director | Alice Briggs

ADVERTISING & MARKETING

Inquiries
Ads@AtheniaCreative.com

Information
https://IndieAuthorMagazine.com/
advertising/

CONTRIBUTORS

Angela Archer, Elaine Bateman, Patricia Carr, Bradley Charbonneau, Honorée Corder, Jackie Dana, Heather Clement Davis, Jamie Davis, Laurel Decher, Fatima Fayez, Gill Fernley, Greg Fishbone, Jen B. Green, Jac Harmon, Marion Hermannsen, Steve Higgs, Chrishaun Keller-Hanna, Kasia Lasinska, Monica Leonelle, Jenn Lessmann, Megan Linski-Fox, Craig Martelle, Angie Martin, Merri Maywether, Kevin McLaughlin, Lasairiona McMaster, Jenn Mitchell, Tanya Nellestein, Russell Nohelty, Susan Odev, Eryka Parker, Tiffany Robinson, Clare Sager, Joe Solari, Becca Syme, David Viergutz

SUBSCRIPTIONS
https://indieauthormagazine.com/subscribe/

HOW TO READ
https://indieauthormagazine.com/how-to-read/

WHEN WRITING MEANS BUSINESS
IndieAuthorMagazine.com

Athenia Creative | 6820 Apus Dr., Sparks, NV, 89436 USA | 775.298.1925
ISSN 2768-7880 (online)–ISSN 2768-7872 (print)

Countless craft books and blogs will tell you that the beginning of your book needs to be some of your strongest writing. You have to introduce your narrator and your world and hook your reader into the story, often in a matter of just a few sentences.

In some ways, your book's launch serves the same purpose. Each new story you share with the world has the potential to reach new readers and entice them to explore your other titles. You want each launch to be as strong as possible, to reach the largest number of readers and to help sustain your business until the next one. This month, Joe Solari of Author Nation kicks off his newest column by exploring how to do just that.

Perfecting your launch isn't the be-all and end-all of your book's success, and there are certainly countless strategies to try, some of which may resonate better with your readers than others. But having a strong start undoubtedly makes a difference.

Of course, the metaphor fizzles out at a certain point. Some of you would probably argue that writing an intriguing first line is much easier than keeping track of everything that goes into a book launch—there's a reason IAM's Maria Connor crafted a checklist to help you stay organized. Others may point out that your book's first line has to do a lot more heavy lifting; if you can't snag a reader during your book's launch, they may still fall in love with your writing years after you published it. Michael La Ronn offers some ideas for how to make your backlist shine in this month's Ten Tips article.

There is one more comparison worth making, however. Whether you're writing the first words of a new story or tracking those first sales of a new book, that beginning is worth celebrating. It's the start of the next step in your author journey.

Nicole Schroeder
Editor in Chief
Indie Author Magazine

Nicole Schroeder is a storyteller at heart. As the editor in chief of Indie Author Magazine, she brings nearly a decade of journalism and editorial experience to the publication, delighting in any opportunity to tell true stories and help others do the same. She holds a bachelor's degree from the Missouri School of Journalism and minors in English and Spanish. Her previous work includes editorial roles at local publications, and she's helped edit and produce numerous fiction and nonfiction books, including a Holocaust survivor's memoir, alongside independent publishers. Her own creative writing has been published in national literary magazines. When she's not at her writing desk, Nicole is usually in the saddle, cuddling her guinea pigs, or spending time with family. She loves any excuse to talk about Marvel movies and considers National Novel Writing Month its own holiday.

MARTELLE'S MOTIVATION

Be Your Own Hero

2023 could have been better, but I'm a big fan of the continuous improvement mindset. What did I do right that sets me up for this year? What do I need to improve on?

I take responsibility for my own actions. I got sick. I survived. I changed my forward trajectory. I focused on finishing stuff to open up the future and do more of what is working.

As you look at the year that's finished and the one that's still ahead of you, put out your dumpster fire, and start the year with the smell of smoke and firefighting foam. Add some incense to appeal to your palate. And own what was—and is—in your control.

Don't be a victim in your own story. Be the hero. That means you need to do hero stuff. Don't let the villains win.

Rush into 2024 with a mindset of achievement, of lifting yourself higher than you were before. 2024 is likely going to be a year of negative messaging; each year has its fair share of that. But choose to rise above that with your books to give people a place to escape the shrieking voices and noise of rending metal, of a world crashing down around your shoulders. Then go about being you and doing what's best for you and your business.

Write stories that take people away. Write stories with winners. Write your story, where you're the hero.

Don't write yourself to be the victim, or you risk staring forever at the dark side of every cloud.

It's a new dawn. It's a new day. It will be what you make of it.

Peace, fellow humans. ■

Craig Martelle

Craig Martelle

High school Valedictorian enlists in the Marine Corps under a guaranteed tank contract. An inauspicious start that was quickly superseded by excelling in language study. Contract waived, a year at the Defense Language Institute to learn Russian and off to keep my ears on the big red machine during the Soviet years. Earned a four-year degree in two years by majoring in Russian Language. My general staff. career included choice side gigs – UAE, Bahrain, Korea, Russia, and Ukraine.

Major Martelle. I retired from the Marines after a couple years at the embassy in Moscow working arms control issues.

Department of Homeland Security then law school next. I was working for a high-end consulting firm performing business diagnostics, business law, and leadership coaching. For the money they paid me, I was good with that. Just until I wasn't. Then I started writing.

ALLI EXCLUSIVE

Go for Launch

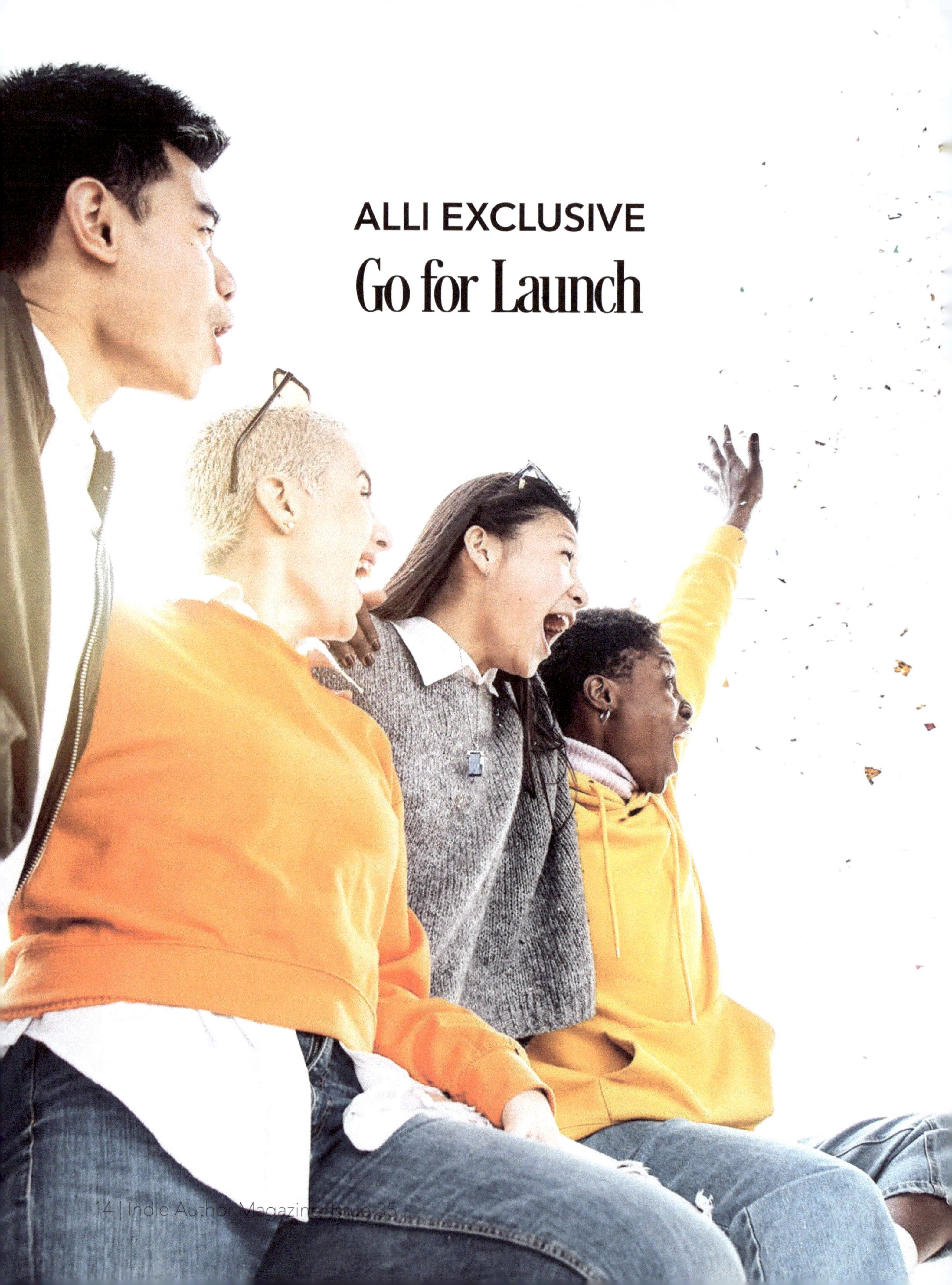

When we use the term "book launch," we're referring to all the planned marketing activities surrounding your new book in its first weeks or months.

The most well-known and popular ways of drawing attention to a new book include

- email marketing, including igniting a reader team and ARC team;
- podcasts and radio;
- mainstream media coverage;
- social media campaigns;
- hosting a launch party and other events, online and off;
- book signings; and
- real-life and virtual book tours.

Often, indie authors think a book launch is one of the most important, if not the most important, part of their marketing campaign. It's the most public and well-known part of the marketing process, often depicted as glamorous affairs during which members of the literati gather and toast the author, who's busy signing hardbacks and taking photos with a long line of adoring fans.

That type of book launch works for authors aiming to sell in physical bookstores, but most indie authors will sell most of their books online. Although physical book launches can be a good marketing tool, indie authors can afford to de-emphasize them and keep a sense of proportion when it comes to our creative time and energies.

We know a book is new to a reader the day they discover it, even if it was published many moons ago. We will continue to market our books before and after the launch period, long after a third-party publisher has moved on to a new author.

See the Alliance of Independent Authors's (ALLi's) ultimate guide to book launches, including a comprehensive timeline and ideas both lavish and budget, at: https://selfpublishingadvice.org/ultimate-guide-to-launching-a-book. Meanwhile, for whatever stage you're at, here are some extra tips.

BEGINNER AUTHORS

For beginner authors who have yet to build up loyal readers, book sales are unlikely to begin at all until they start marketing. This may sound depressing, but actually what it does is give you breathing space, so make the most of it. Take a tip from the world of new product development and "soft launch" first, to make sure everything is in place. Publish the book, but don't tell anyone until you're happy everything has gone successfully: the right version of the book is published, retail platforms are displaying it nicely, and you've found and corrected the inevitable annoying typos.

I've spoken to many new authors who are panicking because they've arranged paid promotions or in-person book launches but have then had some relatively minor and common hiccup occur that threatens to derail their plans. In March 2023, team members with the Alliance of Independent Authors (ALLi) spoke on the organization's podcast about the benefits of a soft launch. Listen to the episode at: https://selfpublishingadvice. org/soft-launching-a-book.

EMERGING AUTHORS

As you settle into a writing and publishing pattern, consider what best suits your creative process.

We can't talk about launch strategies without mentioning the "rapid release" approach, in which authors write and release books very fast, sometimes even monthly, thus keeping their readers constantly satisfied and being buoyed by the retail algorithms, which favor newly released books.

Authors taking this approach either write consistently and quickly between releases or write for an intense period up front and, only once they've finished several books or even a complete series, release each one across a carefully managed rapid-release schedule. There are pros and cons to this style of publishing, and it does rely on an author being able to write quickly while maintaining the quality their readers expect of them. You can read ALLI's guide to this approach here: https://selfpublishingadvice.org/ successful-rapid-release-strategies-for-indie-authors.

But not all of us are such fast writers, and there are many ways to be successful. In ALLi's September 2023 blog post, "Successful Slow-Release Strategies for Indie Authors," we look at how releasing books more slowly can also be a valid approach.

The most obvious benefit of slow-releasing is that it offers authors more time to develop and write each book, either in a series or as stand-alones. This can suit those writers looking to work at a slower pace on each book, either for practical or creative reasons, as well as those who find the launch process of a new book to be time-consuming or stressful.

Building a launch team can be where the more established author really steps up their impact. Sending out ARC copies to a committed reader team and having established relationships with editorial review outlets, not to mention growing a group of loyal readers ready to buy, can make the launch process smoother and more reliable with each new title released. Look through each stage of your usual launch and see what tweaks you can make to raise your game for next time.

New formats of a book can act as mini-launches for that title as a whole. For example, when you bring out an audiobook, you can use elements of it to market the paperback and e-book. Try asking your narrator to record a little extra piece of text that you can use in a book trailer, so your marketing efforts have an additional piece of material to use.

EXPERIENCED AUTHORS

Experienced authors tend to have settled on a process that suits them and have a tried-and-tested approach to launching a book, having done it many times over.

At this stage, having a first round of direct sales to your loyal readers is a good way to launch a book, as it maximizes your profit margins before you focus on other retail platforms. Kickstarter can also be a good way to launch a book or any special projects, as you'll have a committed audience to sell into, and their enthusiasm will add momentum to your campaign. Brandon Sanderson's $41 million Kickstarter for four books may have been a record-breaker, but when you look more closely, it actually reflects a well-established author who could draw on both his previous Kickstarter campaign experience and the enthusiasm of devoted readers.

Finally, remember that one of the perks of self-publishing is that you can relaunch a book at any time. You can re-edit, commission a new cover, write a new blurb, publish a reader magnet linked to it, or start a new advertising campaign. Any or all of these can reinvigorate a book and bring it to the attention of readers again for the first time.

Your book is always new to a new reader; next month, we'll be covering this concept in more detail when we talk about making the most of your backlist. ■

Melissa Addey, ALLi Campaigns Manager

Melissa Addey, ALLI's Campaign Manager

The Alliance of Independent Authors (ALLi) is a global membership association for self-publishing authors. A non-profit, our mission is ethics and excellence in self-publishing. Everyone on our team is a working indie author and we offer advice and advocacy for self-publishing authors within the literary, publishing and creative industries around the world. www.allianceindependentauthors.org

SOLARI SAYS...

Beware the Launch Trough

As authors, creative freedom and administrative responsibilities can sometimes feel like they're at odds with each other, and understanding the publishing industry can pose a challenge to even the most strategy-savvy authors. But there's no need to figure it out alone. In his new quarterly column, Managing Director of Author Nation and business expert Joe Solari shares his observations and tips for mastering the administrative side of your author career. When you write like you mean business, your writing can become one—just consider what Solari says.

Your publishing business is like a collection of book launches. Making sure each launch is successful will have a positive impact on your overall business. However, there is a challenge you need to be aware of. I call it the launch trough. And if you are a new author, this will be more daunting, as you have no history to help you plan how to cross it.

The launch trough refers to the investment you must make when launching a book. This includes production and marketing costs to bring the book to market. It also involves considering the time value of money, such as when you need to invest it and when you expect to recover it. The depth of the launch trough refers to how much money you have to spend, and the duration is the time it takes to recover all the money spent. The depth and duration of the launch trough determine the financial challenge you will face. The key to success is to cross this trough quickly.

The best solution is to have savings to cover it. For example, if the launch trough lasts six weeks and requires $3,000, it is advisable to save that amount ahead of time to sustain you during the launch. If you have a multiple-release strategy, such as releasing the first two books in a series six weeks apart, the depth of the trough increases to $6,000, and the potential trough duration could extend to eighteen weeks.

How could it be so long? If this is a new series and releasing multiple books is required to demonstrate to your audience that you are committed to the series and it is worth their time, sales won't ramp up until the other books are released.

IT'S NOT ALWAYS UP AND TO THE RIGHT

Publishing is a cyclical business. By the very nature of your product release being tied to your capacity to put books out and your existing audience's ability to consume those books, you will see ups and downs.

I have looked at thousands of book launches while helping authors with their businesses. My observation is that every book launch follows a steep decline as the existing audience is exhausted. The single biggest driver of sales will be your existing audience. But the bigger that audience, the bigger the highs and the steeper the drop.

In one example, an initial peak in month two—created by authors releasing books at the end of a month to capture preorder sales—is followed by a steep drop, where sales settle out to a level supported by organic discovery and purchases. An observable trend across authors, genres, and levels of popularity is that 80 percent of a title's sales happen in the first ten months.

This buy-and-binge mentality is the strongest, most reliable driver of visibility. Sales recommendation engines determine the acute buying behavior and look to reproduce it by showing your new book to similar people. Some of those will be your invisible audience who buy just that book, and others will be introduced to you and buy the first book in the series.

To ensure the success of your book launches, it's best to have a system to attract new readers and make the most of the visibility gained during the launch. The simplest system is to have the offer of bonus material, like an epilogue or cut-out scene offered in the back of your first book in exchange for an email. Those that go to your first book, read it, and like it will sign up, filling your mailing list with organic readers.

Here is an example from another author in a different genre. *The Blue Line* is the first book in a series. With this book, the author experienced a steep initial curve and several pops of sales with subsequent releases in the series. This author has a good retention system designed to get those new readers into the series and move through subsequent books. If you can design a series of bonus offers that gets readers to keep signing in, your readers will move through your backlist and stay intrigued about what's coming next.

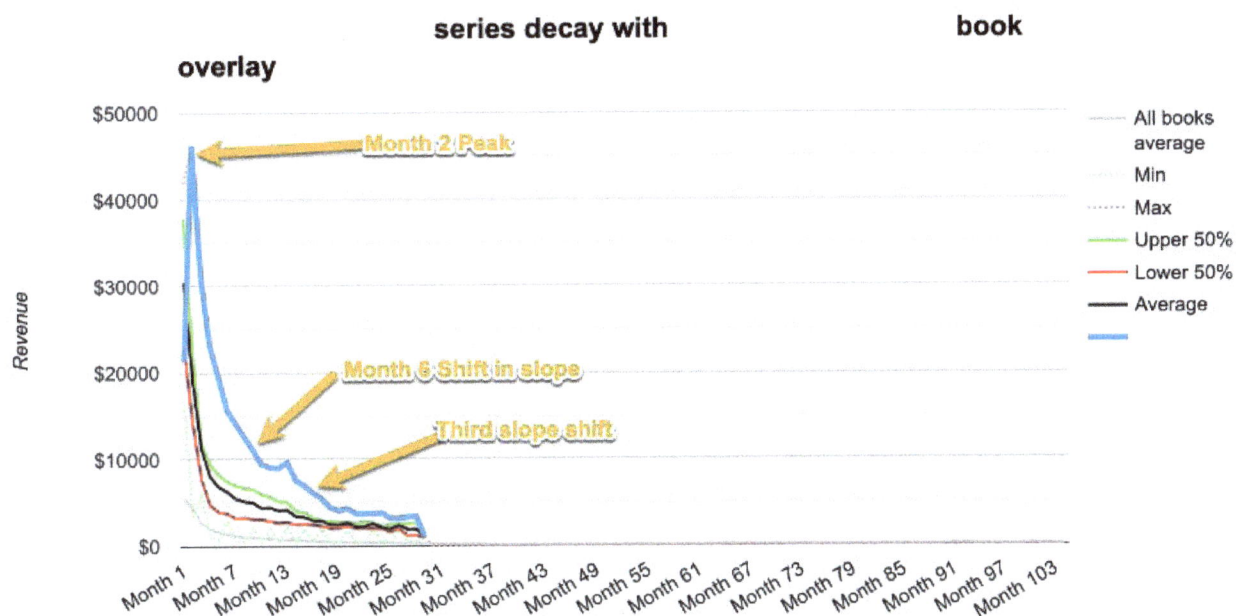

Specific series decay data

Select series _____
Select book to overlay on decay series decay chart

series decay with book overlay

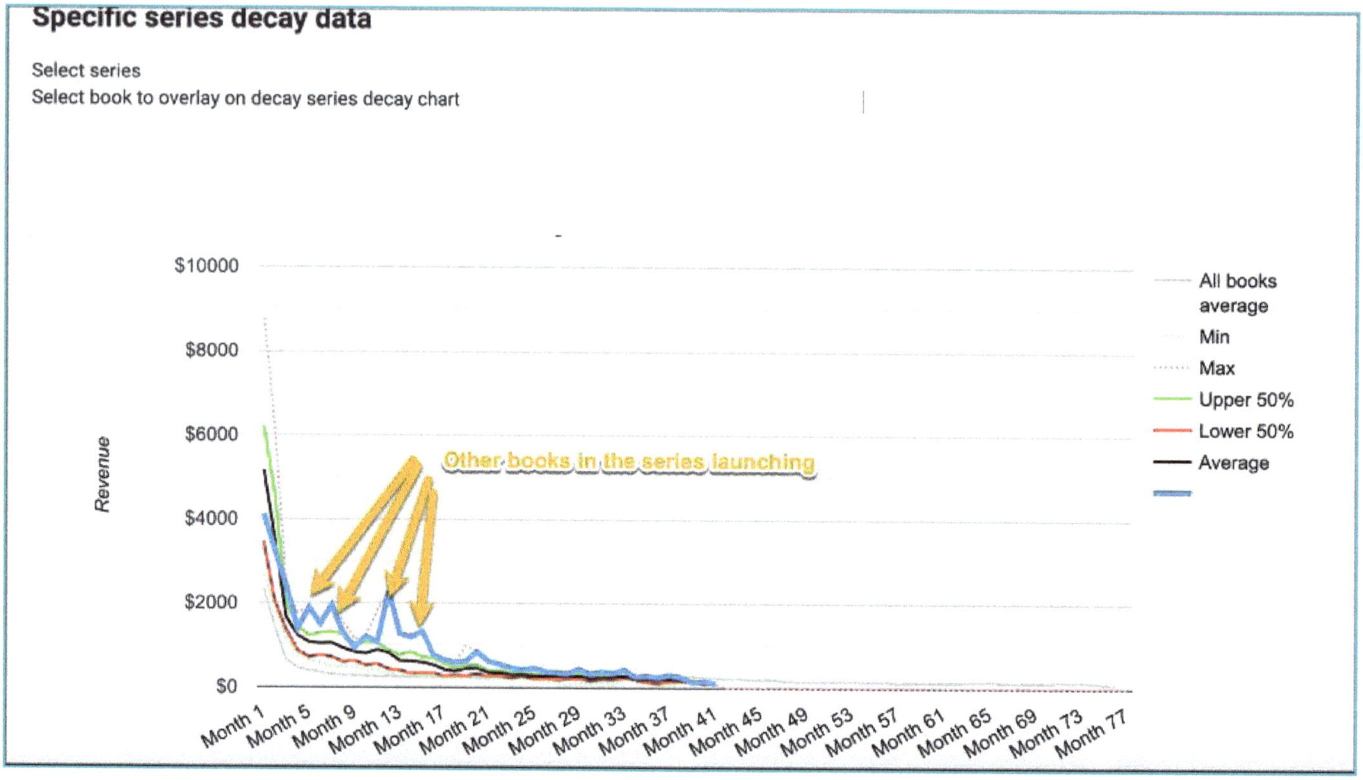
Specific series decay data
Select series
Select book to overlay on decay series decay chart
Revenue
$10000
$8000
$6000
$4000
$2000
$0
Other books in the series launching
All books average
Min
Max
Upper 50%
Lower 50%
Average
Month 1
Month 5
Month 9
Month 13
Month 17
Month 21
Month 25
Month 29
Month 33
Month 37
Month 41
Month 45
Month 49
Month 53
Month 57
Month 61
Month 65
Month 69
Month 73
Month 77

WHAT SHOULD YOU DO?

I've studied thousands of launch curves and done analyses of the monthly sales. This has led to some practices that can result in better results now and increase the success of future launches.

Don't fight the curve. Trying to sustain a certain sales level through advertising can result in a less profitable business. Embrace the cyclicality, and design your launch plan and business around bringing in money in short periods and conserving funds to get you through to the next launch. Pay closer attention to where sales plateau after a launch. Give more credence to higher valleys than higher peaks. The speed of releases isn't as important as the regularity of the release. If you write slower, just make it clear to your audience how often to expect a book.

Have a system to attract new readers. When your book gains attention during its launch, new readers who come across it may decide to make a purchase. If your book is part of a series, they might even go back to the first book and buy that. It's important to have ways to directly connect with your audience, such as through email, and to have systems in place to guide them through your other books at their own pace. These two factors play a significant role in the success of future book launches, even more so than any amount of advertising you may do.

Understand the numbers. By keeping track of the financial aspects of each book launch, you can better manage your overall business. The return from each release and each book's performance in its first six to nine months will give you insights into how quickly you'll start making a profit in your author business.

If you're new to publishing or if your previous launches haven't resulted in a return on investment, it's important to consider how much you're willing to invest in this venture at the outset. It may require more than $10,000 and take up to five years to break even. If it takes longer than six to nine months to turn a profit, it's crucial to reassess your approach. It may be that readers aren't that into your books. Never forget: it is the act of reading your book that sells the reader on your brand.

If you're new to this, here are some more simple steps to track your progress:

Make a list of all the costs associated with the book launch, including production and marketing expenses.

Add up these costs and multiply the total by 1.1 to account for a 10 percent return on investment.

Divide this amount by the royalties you receive from book sales or page reads if you sell on Kindle Select. Consider the percentage of revenue that comes from page reads to determine the number of pages needed to reach 70 percent of your return on investment.

This will give you a target to aim for during the initial phase of your book launch, which typically lasts three to six months.

By understanding the costs involved in each launch and setting realistic goals for return on investment, you can effectively manage your finances and make your publishing business profitable. Remember to stay persistent, adapt to the market, and keep pursuing your passion for writing and publishing. ■

Joe Solari

Joe Solari

Joe Solari is an author, entrepreneur, and consultant. Since 2016 he has been helping best-selling authors build great publishing businesses. He has worked to create tools and systems to help passionate business owners professionalize their team and operations to achieve exceptional results.

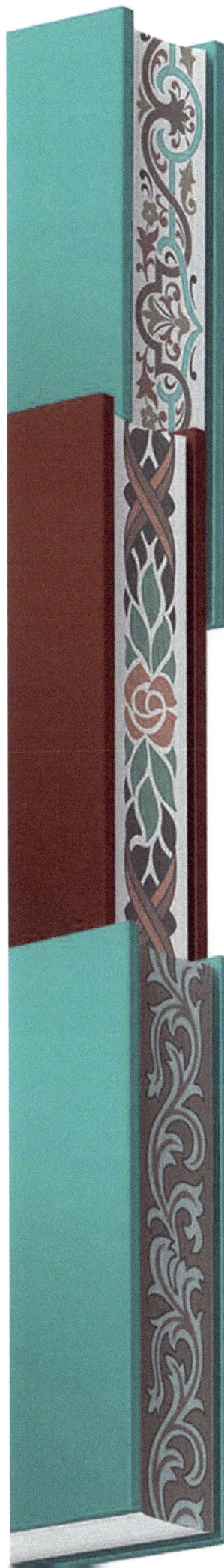

Dear Indie Annie,

I've only ever written in one particular genre. I have an audience built there, a decent backlist, and a few ideas for future books. But I just recently got an idea for a story in an entirely different genre—one that I don't even know I'll continue past this book. Do I write the new idea or stick with what I know?

Pestered by a Plot Bunny

Dearest Plot Bunny,

The temptation of an off-brand manuscript is exciting but risky, like swapping sleek style for avant-garde fashion on a whim. Do you take the plunge or stick to familiar fashions? Let's review strategies to craft your author couture.

First, consider your devoted audience. Passion projects outside your audience's expectations require extra strategy. Will a singular stylistic experiment dilute your hard-earned readership? Will fans of your signature look embrace radical style shifts? Genre pivots may leave loyalists feeling out of fashion.

Is your new genre outside of the broader interests of your current readership? If so, consider pen names to keep your brand distinct, like Nora Roberts separating J.D. Robb thrills from her Romance catalog or Anne Rice crediting her Sleeping Beauty Erotica series to the pseudonym A.N. Roquelaure, thereby keeping styles separate.

Growth requires expanding horizons, I hear you cry! I agree. As Emerson said, "All life is an experiment." However, I urge you to listen carefully to your favorite writing auntie. Yes, it is important to follow your creative bliss, but from a business stance, I suggest you do so in moderation. Ease into new genres subtly, accessorizing with familiar elements. Infuse expected flavors to make surprises wearable. And above all, limit your vanity writing to time you can afford without losing momentum on the primary projects your fans crave. Find a sustainable work-life—or rather business head-creative muse—balance.

Balance is crucial. Sketch a career plan before you pivot patterns. Can your workroom handle multiple creative lines? Limit works-in-progress so you don't lose focus. Remember, leaving signature

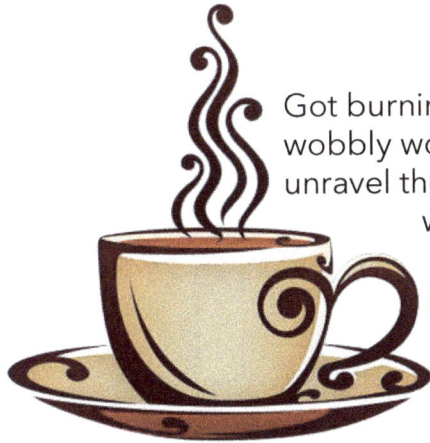

Got burning questions about the wibbly-wobbly world of indie authoring? Eager to unravel the mysteries of publishing, writing woes, or anything in between? Give your quizzical quills a whirl and shoot your musings over to indieannie@ indieauthormagazine.com. Your inky quandaries are my cup of tea!

styles untouched for too long risks fans seeking alternate providers of their much-loved staples.

As always, I suggest you track data to guide your decisions. Survey fans on their genre interests. Check sales metrics on your backlist stories. Where is reader demand trending? Lean into what sells while judiciously branching out. Beware drastic departures without a roadmap. Consider how, my dear one, after beloved satires like *A Confederacy of Dunces*, John Kennedy Toole tragically lost his voice attempting darker character studies. Maintain your unique creative compass.

With that warning ringing in your ears, if you do not want to have a separate pen name, set expectations by announcing your outlier endeavor as loud as you can. Subtitle new-genre stories to signpost your readers to the change, with something like "A Sci-Fi Story," for example. Craft thoughtful messaging contextualizing how this new venture fits within your wider vision as an author. Ensure your covers are setting your readers up for the different tales inside. But

above all, reassure your readers that you aren't abandoning the genres and stories they love.

The next step, of course, is to create thoughtful social media and newsletter messages to announce your different direction. Even use your newsletter to put the call out for beta readers who may be there, lurking in the shadows. Above all, make change digestible.

So yes, my little fashionista, dress your spirit! But evolve strategically, not through blind impulse. Passion projects warrant extra caution to avoid derailing professional publishing plans. With mindful balancing, you can achieve enduring success! As Kafka said, "Don't bend; don't edit your soul according to fashion." But evolve wisely, with an eye on your vision.

This look requires careful thought, darling one! Harmonize habits and adventurousness, and you'll be a timeless couturier.

Happy writing,
Indie Annie X

10 TIPS FOR
REVITALIZING YOUR BACKLIST

Your backlist is a vital part of your author career because it's always available. A book you wrote ten years ago may seem like old news to you, but it will be just as fresh as it was on launch day to readers who find it today.

Backlists take the pressure off grueling production schedules for new titles. The bigger your backlist, the more money you can earn. However, it's normal to feel overwhelmed by the idea of refreshing your backlist. The process can take time and effort—but it doesn't have to be hard.

You can approach revitalizing your backlist in three steps:

1. Review your books.
2. Review your marketing materials.
3. Send traffic to your backlist.

Read on for ten tips to get the best out of your backlist with little time, effort, and money.

STEP 1: REVIEW YOUR BOOKS

1 ASSESS YOUR BOOK COVER

Older book covers might need a redesign, but consider the cost, especially with a large backlist. According to the book cover design company MiblArt, common mistakes with cover designs include bad fonts, bland designs, and poor image quality. New authors often make these mistakes. Identify bestselling self-published books in your subgenre that were published after your book so you can spot new trends. You should look at self-published books because their covers are most likely to be appealing to your target readers. You can also use tools like K-Lytics (https://K-Lytics.com) and Publisher Rocket (https://PublisherRocket.com) to do market research and find comparable books quickly.

Pro Tip: Place your book cover with ten recent best-selling indie covers on a Pinterest board. If it blends in, rebranding might not be necessary. If it doesn't, consider a rebrand. Send the Pinterest board to your designer, and ask them to design something that fits on the board.

(2) SPRUCE UP YOUR BOOK DESCRIPTION

Unlike cover design, rewriting your book description is free and may help grab potential readers' attention just as effectively.

According to BookBub, it's important to keep your specific genre in mind as you write your sales copy. Pay careful attention to the language that indie bestsellers in your category use in their descriptions, and analyze your book description against comparable books, carefully reviewing the hook and first paragraph in particular. Also be sure to include sales words, like "captivating," "spell-binding," and "full throttle." You can even consider adding snippets from reviews to your book description—all of it helps to build hype for your book.

While you're here, don't forget to refresh the metadata for your book. Look at your categories and keywords to see if they need updating.

Pro Tip: Use AI tools like ChatGPT or Claude for rewriting tips. They can help you find hidden opportunities to use more sales words, making your description more appealing.

(3) REVAMP YOUR BACK MATTER

In your back matter, consider an Other Books By page to promote your most popular backlist titles. If you have a small backlist, you may have to update this page from time to time as you release new books, but an outdated page is still better than no page at all.

If your backlist contains series that are different from your current one, sending readers to those backlist books can be a good way of keeping them entertained until you launch the next book in your active series, especially if you don't release new work quickly.

STEP 2: REVIEW YOUR MARKETING MATERIALS

(4) ADAPT YOUR AUTORESPONDERS

Autoresponders are a series of pre-written emails that are sent to your mailing list in response to specific triggers, like new signups. Most email marketing platforms allow you to create them.

The Alliance of Independent Authors recommends updating your autoresponder sequence to inform readers about your backlist. They also recommend adding to your autoresponder sequence each time you release a new book or series.

⑤ EXPAND INTO NEW EDITIONS

Your book is likely to exist as an e-book and trade paperback, but consider the following additional formats:

- hardcover (case laminate or dust jacketed);
- limited edition hardcovers, with a foil-stamped cover, illustrations, or custom chapter headers;
- large print; or
- audiobooks or translations, if your books are selling well and you have the money.

These editions are easier to create than ever before now that many cover designers are familiar with them and IngramSpark no longer charges setup fees.

Pro Tip: Consider launching a Kickstarter campaign to help you fund the creation of these editions. While time-intensive, Kickstarter is a great way to drum up renewed interest in older books.

⑥ CREATE COVER MOCKUPS

Use a tool like Book Brush (https://BookBrush.com) to create compelling mockups of your books that you can share on social media. These tools allow you to put your book on mocked-up tablets, phones, and even paperback books. Mockups are more eye-catching on social media feeds than flat book cover images and may draw more eyes to your promotional posts.

You can also use Book Brush to create ads for Facebook and BookBub Ads, so it can serve a dual purpose in your revitalization efforts.

STEP 3: SEND TRAFFIC TO YOUR BACKLIST

⑦ UPDATE YOUR WEBSITE

Consider spotlighting a featured backlist title or series on your website's homepage, just below the fold—before users have to scroll. The homepage is often the most visited page on a website, so it is prime real estate to promote your backlist.

Find other creative ways to promote your backlist on your website, such as in the menu bar of your blog, the footers of your blog posts, or a dedicated page for each of your books or series on your website's navigation menu.

⑧ WRITE A NEWSLETTER

It's easy to overlook your newsletter, so if you haven't communicated with your readers recently, run a $0.99 promotion and send a quick email to your readers to let them know about it.

Keep your email brief, but be sure to include your new cover if you have one, your revised book description, and any creative mockups. Remind your audience about your backlist every so often—if anyone is newer to your mailing list, they might not realize you have other books available until you tell them.

9 RUN ADS

Ads can be a great way to test your rebranding efforts. Experiment with small-budget ad campaigns on Amazon, Facebook, and BookBub. If you're active on TikTok, consider ads there as well.

If you're not familiar with these ad platforms, consider investing in a paid course to learn the basics quickly. Although these platforms have a learning curve, you will have lessened your work considerably if you have a new cover, revised book description, and creative mockups.

You can also stack promotions with a $0.99 sale using sites like CraveBooks (https://CraveBooks.com) to help you get more out of your promotion campaign.

10 SELL DIRECT

Selling books directly on your site can also help your backlist sales. Whether you sell on Payhip (https://Payhip.com), Gumroad (https://Gumroad.com), Shopify (https://Shopify.com), or a similar direct sales platform, you can create special offers for your readers.

With the increasing popularity of tools like BookFunnel (https://BookFunnel.com) and StoryOrigin (https://StoryOriginApp.com) delivering books directly to readers, many readers are more familiar with purchasing books direct from authors. Selling direct is a great way to increase your income.

Use direct sales platforms to offer special coupons and upsells that you can't create on retailer sites. For example, you might offer a 10 percent Christmas coupon, or, if a reader buys book 1 in a series, you might upsell them books 2 and 3 at a small discount.

Pro Tip: Use a printer like Bookvault (https://Bookvault.app) to enable direct print sales on your website. Bookvault integrates with Shopify, and when readers purchase the book, it ships directly from Bookvault, and you don't have to keep inventory.

You don't have to do all of this in one day. Take it one step at a time, and you'll be well on your way to revitalizing your backlist, growing your income, and keeping your books fresh for years to come. Your backlist will thank you!

Michael La Ronn

Michael La Ronn

Michael La Ronn has published over 80 science fiction & fantasy books and self-help books for writers. He built a writing career publishing 10-12 books per year while raising a family, working a full-time job, and even attending law school classes in the evenings. He is also the Outreach Manager at the Alliance of Independent Authors, a nonprofit organization for self-published writers. Visit his fiction website at www.michaellaronn.com and his resources for writers at www.authorlevelup.com.

Traveling through the Fog

JONATHAN YAÑEZ ON WRITING INTO THE DARK AND TAKING THE NEXT STEP

Jonathan Yañez doesn't have an outline. Some authors talk about writing by the Headlight Method, plotting only as far down the road as their headlights will shine. For Jonathan, assuming that the lights are on might give him too much credit—by his own account. The internationally bestselling author, filmmaker, and entrepreneur will admit to having "a general sense of an idea of where I want the story to go—maybe four or five points." But for the most part, when he starts writing or takes on a new project, the path forward is about as clear as it was the day he quit his job in 2012.

"All I could see was the next step ahead of me," he says. With no backup plan, and without discussing it with his wife first, Jonathan walked away from a sales and marketing position he'd held for five years and became a full-time writer. "My whole career has been a lot of faith—just blind faith—and taking that next step and hoping and praying that that step is going to be there when I land."

The risks have more than paid off.

Unsure of anything beyond the fact that he hated his job and couldn't see a healthy future there, Jonathan shifted into a new career as an author. He took a part-time position as a personal trainer to help pay the bills and immediately started doing what he loved: writing. Eight months later, he had a completed manuscript and eighty query rejections. The next query letter resulted in an agent and a traditional publishing deal for a series of books based on his debut novel, a Young Adult Urban

WOLF PACK
ENTERTAINMENT

Fantasy called *The Beast Within*.

By 2014, he'd published five books traditionally and two independently. When he saw the success of his independent novels and the difference in net royalties, he left his publisher.

Jonathan has no complaints about his traditional publishing experience, and indeed, he may soon return to traditional publishing as a hybrid author. But "I saw what they were doing, and I understood that I was capable of doing the same thing," he says.

CHARTING A PATH

Jonathan says he soon realized the quickest way to build an audience was to put out as much content as he could as soon as he could. So he built a routine that allowed him to publish eight to twelve books per year. He does most of his writing in sprints: one thousand words in twenty to thirty minutes, four times a day, six days a week, resulting in about eighty thousand finished words per month. When he sits down to work, he says, "I already know exactly what I'm going to write. I've been thinking about it. I've been dreaming about it." But his dreams still only go as far as what he intends to write the next day.

The routine has shifted a little as his family and business have grown. Jonathan and his wife, Jynafer, now have two small children, and the Yañez brand has expanded. Jynafer followed Jonathan's lead, leaving her job in marketing to take over running the family business. He calls her "the CEO," and she refers to him as "the Talent." They split the responsibilities of their business with those of raising their two children. According to Jonathan, on a typical day, "I wake up at 5 a.m., and I write until 1 p.m. We homeschool our kids, so from five to one, my wife is with the kids, and then in the afternoons,

it's her time to work. So I'm with the kids from one until about four or five. Then we have family time until about seven, when the kids go to bed. So from eight to nine, my wife and I get to spend time together." He's in bed by 9 p.m.

Although this schedule made him a successful author, once he got comfortable with the business of writing and selling books, Jonathan started looking for new ways to grow. He says that he always wants to be "grateful for everything but hungry for more."

To that end, Jonathan approaches his life the same way he writes his books: with just a few mile markers in sight. He writes a list of five things he wants to accomplish "some day." Each year he consults the list, checks off the goals that have been met, and adds new ones. He says that in the beginning of his career, he could never have imagined some of the things that he's accomplished, but by challenging himself this way, he forces himself to grow. "If that seems impossible, if we want to dream bigger, we should do that," he says of choosing goals that seem just out of reach.

CHANGING DIRECTIONS

After finding success in independent publishing, Jonathan's next step into the darkness led to visions of marquee lights. About three years ago, while researching successful authors who'd transitioned to different media, Jonathan discovered that Michael Crichton once had the number one bestselling book, number one movie, and number one TV show in the same year.

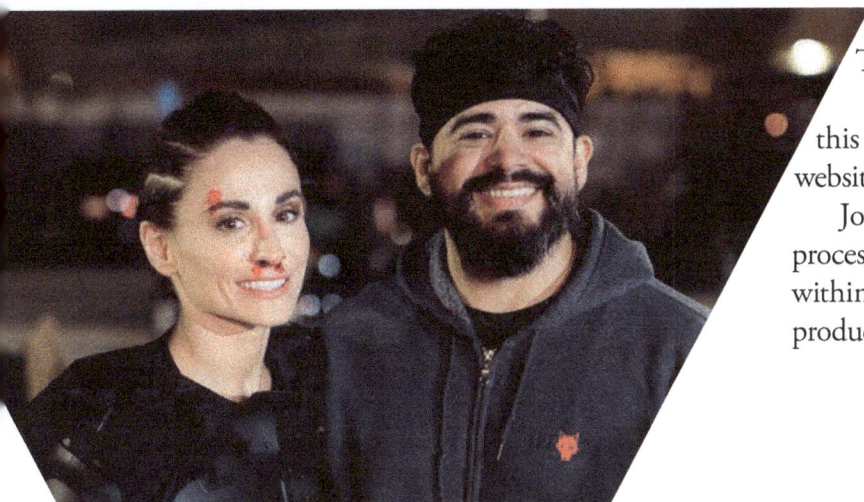

According to *Vanity Fair*, Crichton has held this distinction multiple times, and his author website asserts that he's the only one to have done so.

Jonathan started looking into the filmmaking process and started networking to build connections within the industry. For his first project, he wrote and produced a pilot episode for an original Space Western television show. His production company started work in January 2021, launched a Kickstarter in October 2021—which fully funded in nine days—filmed over five days in January 2022, and premiered in June 2022. The project, *Infinity System*, wracked up over one hundred thousand views on YouTube, won film festival awards, and earned the attention of both a literary agent and an entertainment lawyer. Jonathan has since completed a short book series based on the pilot, which he hopes to publish traditionally and then option for film.

Fans of his independently published Forsaken Mercenary book series, many of whom backed the *Infinity System* project, turned out again when Jonathan set up his second Kickstarter. This time, he wanted to bring his already bestselling book to the big screen. Offering perks like set visits, red carpet events, signed posters, and challenge coins, the *Forsaken Mercenary* film funded in twenty-nine hours.

Jonathan observes that the writing process for film is easier than for books, though he continues to publish four to six books a year between new projects. Since scripts are significantly shorter, he's found the transition in style and format to be mostly a matter of research and practice. "The easiest way for me to learn a different skill set is just to do it—to practice it and do it over and over and over again," he says.

Likewise, Jynafer has taken on new roles, co-producing both films and directing *Forsaken Mercenary*. She also organizes signings and arranges meet-ups with their reader community, the Wolf Pack. "I just want to be sure that I take all of these readers and people who have supported me throughout the years along with me on this journey," Jonathan says. That means checking in with their Facebook group, hosting Facebook Lives, and responding to readers' requests. Jonathan proudly wears the Wolf Pack logo in interviews and has made sure to incorporate reader feedback when developing new products.

LIGHTING THE WAY FORWARD

As for what comes next, Jonathan shared one of the big goals on his checklist: owning his own studio. He looks forward to having more control of his own projects, a sentiment that drew him to indie publishing in the first place. He'll continue to publish stories of redemption and hope, now as a hybrid author and filmmaker, and see where the next step takes him. Although Jonathan hasn't put a plan in place to match Crichton's accomplishment—it's too far down the road, he says—he advises other authors to "dream bigger sooner," and says he "would encourage them not to put a limit on themself.

"Whatever you decide to do, just make sure you love it and then work to be the best at it. That's it," he says.

Sometimes the next step is hard to see, but he pushes forward anyway. "The number one rule is not to give up," he says. "If God's taught me anything, it's just: don't give up. Even on the days that you feel your worst, even if you can just get back up, that's enough on those days. As long as you don't give up, you will get there." ■

Jenn Lessmann

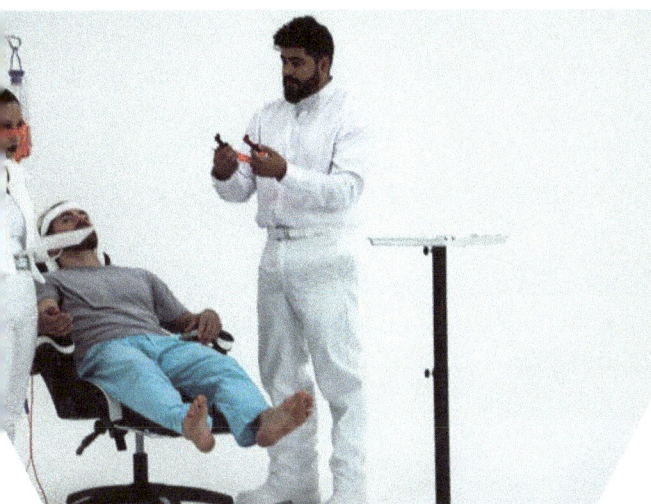

Jenn Lessman

Jenn Lessmann is the author of Unmagical: a Witchy Mystery and three stories on Kindle Vella. A former barista, stage manager, and high school English teacher with advanced degrees from impressive colleges, she continues to drink excessive amounts of caffeine, stay up later than is absolutely necessary, and read three or four books at a time. Jenn is currently studying witchcraft and the craft of writing, and giggling internally whenever they intersect.

Unlocking the Power of Podcast Appearances for Authors

I did not go out to find podcasts as an author. Strangely enough, podcasts found me.

During the early months of the 2020 pandemic, I was facing the loss of many in-person appearances and book fairs. Out of the blue, some of my writer friends invited me to join their podcast since they knew I had panel-speaking experience. I did not know what Zoom was. I didn't own a webcam. It is a wonder I got into the recording with my antique laptop. But my friends gave many helpful suggestions along the way about etiquette, equipment, and networking.

Years later, I have a small podcast studio set up in my home office with a 4K webcam, physical backdrop, and additional lighting. It gets plenty of use.

Why is it important for authors to podcast? Just as with in-person appearances, podcasts allow you direct access to diverse audiences. They can enhance your credibility and establish you as an authority in your genre. Podcast episodes remain accessible online, providing a lasting platform for potential listeners to discover your work long after the initial broadcast.

IDENTIFY YOUR TARGET PODCASTS

Podcasts come in all shapes and sizes. More common formats include audio-only podcasts and video-based podcasts that could be set up on an in-person stage, via a video call, or as a prerecorded reading that is assembled by an editor afterward. Some are general literature podcasts with big audiences. These are more mainstream and often more difficult for a new author to land, as the producers of these podcasts seek name recognition from their guests.

Other podcasts specialize in a niche for listeners who are there for specific content. These podcasts are for a certain genre, a specific fandom, or focus on the craft of writing. Approaching podcasts of your genre can be a better choice than a large mainstream podcast because the listeners will be more interested in your book. It is a matter of matching your novel to the listening market.

Think of podcast directories and platforms as your treasure map—X marks the spot where your perfect podcast awaits. Start by diving into popular platforms like Apple Podcasts, Spotify, or Google Podcasts. Each lists thousands of podcasts for you to view and select from, or explore a list of author-specific podcasts at https://indieauthormagazine.com/podcasts. This method takes time, but can allow you the best range of podcasts to approach as a guest.

Pro Tip: Most podcasts are set up on Apple because of early influence by iTunes, so this can be a good platform to begin your search. Type in keywords related to your book and genre. You will discover a list of potential podcasts that match your vibe. It's like online dating for your book—swipe right on the ones that make your author heart skip a beat.

There are also services that act as a "matchmaker" between possible guests and podcast hosts. Some of these services cost a monthly fee, but they can shorten the time it takes to find the perfect podcast for you to appear on.

PodcastGuests
https://podcastguests.com
This service offers a free newsletter that will send you possible matches with podcasts in their service. If you feel you are a good match, they offer you easier access to gain a spot on the podcast.

PodMatch
https://podmatch.com
This service works similar to a dating service, but instead of finding the right mate, it helps you discover the right podcast to appear on. You create a profile in their service, and the algorithm sends you possibilities. You connect with the podcaster via their in-house message service. PodMatch charges users a monthly fee.

Matchmaker.fm
https://www.matchmaker.fm
This service matches you with podcasts based on your interest categories. You can start with a free account, then move to a paid version with more features.

RESEARCH POTENTIAL PODCASTS

Listen to a few episodes of shows you're interested in before you hit up a podcast producer for a guest spot. You'll get a sneak peek into the way they talk and what makes their audience tick.

Have a clear idea of the type of podcast you are looking for. As you listen to samples, take notes about the audience size, who the producer and host are, their contact information, and any other details you feel are important. This can be found in the podcast's show notes on the podcast's episode page.

CRAFT AN IRRESISTIBLE PITCH

You have selected a list of podcasts you are interested in. Now, it's all about nailing that pitch and making the podcast hosts go, "Yep, we need this author on our show!" Start with a detailed author bio, throw in a general description of your book, and include unique angles in your story that will resonate specifically with their listeners.

Send your inquiry via email to the producer of the podcast you are interested in. Be friendly,

conversational, and highlight how you can be an asset to their program. Remember, podcasters are looking for interesting stories and people. There's no need to send a formal press release to podcasters, but have one ready if they ask for one.

Pro Tip: Consider including personal connections, such as if you've met the show runner at a conference or belong to the same social media group.

BUILD RELATIONSHIPS WITH PODCAST HOSTS

Think of podcast hosts as acquaintances who could become future friends. When you invest time in these relationships, it may result in more than a one-time appearance. Sometimes podcasts form a stable of speakers to draw upon for their various panel shows. Being accepted in such a group can be like gold. Not only do you have future opportunities to appear on the same podcast, but others in the group might also invite you to appear on their own projects.

Use social media to interact with your fellow podcasters. Follow the hosts and panelists, hit them up with genuine comments, and share their podcast projects. Think of podcasting events as networking sites. Collaboration is the magic word; suggest joint projects or guest appearances. Making these connections turns the podcast from marketing to a place to hang out with writer friends.

Pro Tip: Follow podcasts before you become a guest. Sometimes a podcast will post a call on social media. If you are in their circle, you could have early access to this call and get ahead of the competition. For popular podcasts, following them on Instagram, X, or Facebook could be key to landing a spot on their program.

PODCAST EQUIPMENT

You will only need basic equipment to podcast as a guest. Your equipment doesn't need to be expensive; start small and work yourself up to better hardware as you can.

You will need a computer, tablet, or phone to access Zoom. This is the most popular software for video podcasts. You do not need to pay for a Zoom account in order to be a guest podcaster. A free account will gain you access.

Obtain a camera and microphone to record yourself. To start, you can use the built-in tools on your phone or laptop. They are not perfect but will get you started. When you're ready to upgrade, look into webcams or a video-capable camera with a quality lens.

Create a quiet location in your home where you can podcast without people walking into your frame and where you have good lighting. A window with natural light is a good choice, but there are also temperature-controlled lamps to brighten a dark room.

Create a pleasing backdrop behind you. You could purchase a backdrop scene and holder, set up a green screen to project a digital background on, or arrange a neat corner of shelves with your favorite decor items.

PODCAST PREP

You have landed a podcast. Congratulations! It is time to prep for your appearance. Practice those key messages until they roll off your tongue like your favorite quote. Have anecdotes ready to sprinkle in. Think of the recording as not just an interview but a chance to share your author journey, and when you step up to that mic, you're not just a guest—you're the storyteller everyone can't wait to listen to.

If your podcast appearance involves a video call, remember to either create a digital background featuring your name and book via your favorite graphic program or have a place to keep your physical book in the shot with you.

Pro Tip: Feeling those pre-podcast jitters? Totally normal! First, embrace your preparation. Outline your topics and have a list of notes handy to refer to as you record. The better you know your material, the more confident you'll feel and sound. Create practice sessions at your microphone to become more comfortable at your recording station. Finally, remember it is okay to make mistakes. Like a musician at a concert, there will be a few misplayed notes. It is nothing to worry about.

At the start of the program, be prepared to introduce yourself to the host and audience. Tell them why you are a good fit for the show, and have a short bio of yourself practiced. At the end of the show, your host will probably ask you to share your social media handles. Have a short list of no more than two prepared. Chances are your podcast host will also list your links in the show notes.

The key takeaway? It's not just about appearing on any podcast; it's about playing the long game, strategically picking shows, and building relationships that make you the go-to author. Your audience awaits, and with the right approach, your podcast journey is bound to be a winner! ■

Wendy Van Camp

Wendy Van Camp

Wendy Van Camp is the Poet Laureate for the City of Anaheim, California. Her work is influenced by cutting edge technology, astronomy, and daydreams. A graduate of the Ad Astra Speculative Fiction Workshop, Wendy is a nominated finalist for the Elgin Award, for the Pushcart Prize, and for a Dwarf Stars Award. Her poems, stories, and articles have appeared in: "Starlight Scifaiku Review", "The Junction", "Quantum Visions", and other literary journals. She is the poet and illustrator of "The Planets: a scifaiku poetry collection" and editor of the annual anthology "Eccentric Orbits: An Anthology of Science Fiction Poetry".

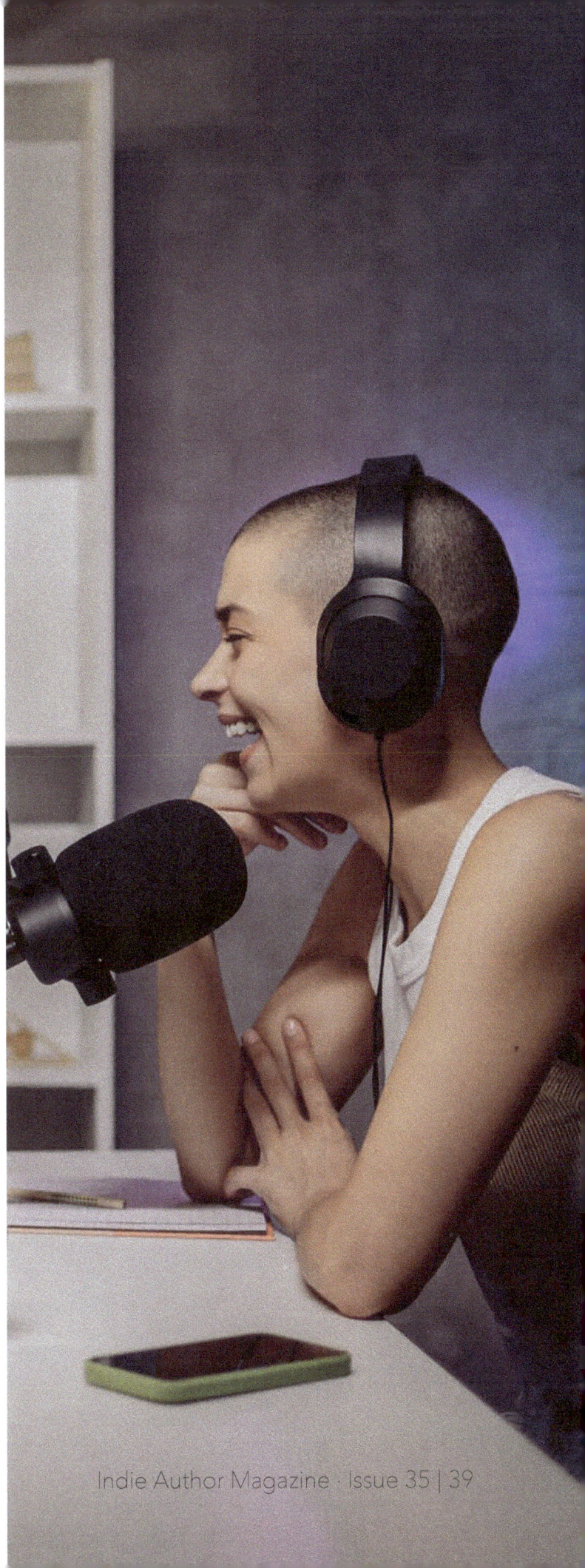

Everything You Need to Know about Running a Virtual Launch Party

Launch parties aren't just a fun way to celebrate your new book release; these events can also be a great way to gain new readers, grow your business, and boost your earnings. And they don't always need a venue or complex setup.

Authors can host virtual launch parties via a series of scheduled posts in a Facebook Group, similar to an author takeover event on social media; a livestream on YouTube, Instagram, or Facebook; or a hosted call on Zoom or similar software. There's no great secret here. Virtual launch parties are simply the online version of an in-person launch party, and they can be just as successful as in-person events while still being tailor made to suit you and your audience.

WHY RUN A VIRTUAL LAUNCH PARTY?

There are many benefits to holding a launch party online.

On the practical side, if you're on a budget, an online party will cost you far less

than an in-person party, both in terms of money and time. There'll be no need to rent a venue or pay for food and drinks. You won't need to order many physical copies of your book unless you're planning on offering signed copies for sale during the launch party. You'll have less physical setup to do, and you and your guests will save on travel costs.

You can also often host a larger event with a virtual party because your guests really can be from anywhere. The only thing to consider is what time of day to have your event, so it's not too early or too late for some attendees.

On the business side, virtual parties can give you the chance to network with other authors in the process of setting up your party and marketing it. Reach out to other authors in your genre to see if they will join your party, offer prizes, or help promote it. You can offer to do the same in return for them. Working together will let you get to know more authors in your genre and find opportunities for further cross-promotion. You'll also reach wider audiences and potentially find new readers.

With a launch party, you'll also get the chance to build your author brand. Place your branding on everything you post leading up to and during your party. This will give a professional look to the whole thing and add to your online reputation.

Your launch party is a great place to promote your backlist. Just because you're running a launch party for a new book doesn't mean you can't talk about other books. Share about related books in the same series or with the same tropes and themes that you want to point people to—just don't overdo it.

SET YOURSELF UP FOR SUCCESS

Launch parties aren't difficult to organize. You just need some time and a checklist to work your way through.

Start by choosing a date that works for your guests and that's as near to your book launch date as you can. You can do a poll or a quick survey to check the best date to hold your party.

Next, think about what you want to get out of your launch party. How many sales would you like to make? How many new newsletter subscribers do you want? What else do you want to achieve? Your answers to these questions should affect the activities you have planned and the way you set up the event—for example, whether you require someone to be signed up for your newsletter to receive an invitation.

Make a list of people you want to invite. Yes, you want mainly readers, but other authors can add a lot to a launch party. They're not your competition, and if they write in the same genre as you, you could pick up some of their audience through the event as they may yours. Consider inviting some influencers and reviewers too, who may do a write-up of your party or a review of your book. Just provide them with a free copy of your book in plenty of time.

Send out your invites in plenty of time so you aren't scrambling for guests or attendees at the last minute. Begin promotion of your event at least a few weeks beforehand. Think about what you can share in your newsletter and on social media to entice people to come. Talk about the other authors who are attending. Run a giveaway for attendees to win a copy of your book and perhaps some swag, and promote that too. When your copies of your book arrive, do an unboxing video and talk about your launch party. What else can you do to promote your event and get people excited about it? Get your ideas down now to give yourself time to implement them.

THE ORDER OF EVENTS

Now that you have your guest list, what should your party include? The lineup is really up to you, but here are a few general ideas:

- an introduction to you and your new book;
- a reading of a couple of enticing excerpts, preferably ending on a cliffhanger;
- a couple of competitions or games to be played during the event, or even a giveaway;
- if your launch party includes a series of posts in a Facebook Group, any appropriate, related memes you can find, or any you make on your own; or
- an author Q&A.

Whatever you're doing, have everything created and ready to go before the event, so you aren't scrambling for what's next. During your party, take your time so you aren't galloping through the event, but don't have too many gaps with nothing happening. It's a balancing act, and you will get better with practice.

FURTHER SUCCESS TIPS

Could you join up with a bookstore in your local area to run a joint event? If bookstores can order your books, the bookstore could buy stock in advance, and you could run your virtual party from their store. This could provide endless opportunities for you as you'll have a better chance of getting future books into that store if your event goes well, and you'll have new contacts in the book world.

Practice! Run through the launch party order and check everything is working, that the order flows, and there aren't any awkward pauses. If you're going to do book readings, practice those too, and make sure you're comfortable with the passages and confident reading them aloud.

Get everything set up in plenty of time so you aren't panicking and rushing at the last minute. Check your internet connection, check your microphones and lights are plugged in and working, and make sure you know what's visible behind you if you're going live. Check your speaking volume and ensure people can hear you.

If you have the budget, consider getting an author banner with your author photo, the launch date, and your book cover. You could even set a stall behind or next to you with physical copies of your books, just like you would if you went to an in-person author event.

Pro Tip: Save money by creating a general, dateless banner featuring more books rather than a specific one just for this book launch. You'll then be able to use it again for other events.

If you can't afford a printed banner, go to town with themed items and props to add atmosphere to your party. For a Regency Romance, you might display a fan and an eye mask from a masked ball, or for a Noir Thriller, you could top your stack of books with a trilby and a magnifying glass.

When you've set the scene, take some photos of your setup and have someone take some of you with your books, back-ground, and props. These will make great promotional images for your newsletter and social posts after the event.

If things go wrong during the event, just roll with it. Most of the time, no one else will notice what should have happened because only you know the running order. Keep calm, don't panic, and you'll still pull off a great launch party.

HOW TO MEASURE YOUR RESULTS

A few days after your event, revisit the goals you set earlier and see how you did. Add up how much the event cost you in terms of promotion and setup. You can then look at your royalties and see whether you covered your costs, or even if you outdid yourself and made quite the profit.

Launch parties are about more than just income, however. Look at statistics like engagement, book sales, KU page reads, new newsletter subscribers and social followers, or new members of your Facebook Group. These new subscribers and followers are available to market to whenever you like.

Send out a short survey a few days after the event to see what people thought and get feedback on how you can improve. You might gain suggestions for other launch parties, feedback on what worked and what didn't, and ways to make your next online launch party an even bigger success.

After all that, pour yourself a glass of something delicious, and celebrate your new book being out in the world. After all, that's what a launch party is about! ■

Gill Fernley

Gill Fernley

Gill Fernley writes fiction in several genres under different pen names, but what all of them have in common is humor and romance, because she can't resist a happy ending or a good laugh. She's also a freelance content writer and has been running her own business since 2013. Before that, she was a technical author and documentation manager for an engineering company and can describe to you more than you'd ever wish to know about airflow and filtration in downflow booths. Still awake? Wow, that's a first! Anyway, that experience taught her how to explain complex things in straightforward language and she hopes it will come in handy for writing articles for IAM. Outside of writing, she's a cake decorator, expert shoe hoarder, and is fluent in English, dry humor and procrastibaking.

IAM's Customizable Countdown Checklist for a Successful Book Launch

You read the how-to book. You borrowed the spreadsheet your author pal created. You invested in the trendy project management software. You have a checklist or three.

Yet every time you launch a book, you cringe—because you forgot to order a cover and realized this when you were uploading the book two hours before the KDP deadline (this really happened), or you neglected to change the price on your free first-in-series, or you never sent out review copies, or you overlooked the email with corrections from your proofreader, or … you get the idea.

Part of the challenge in systematizing the book launch process is that not all releases are created equal. The time, money, and energy you're willing to invest in book 1 of a new series differs from what you'd put behind the re-release of a backlist title or a lead magnet. The strategies employed for Romance differ from those applicable to nonfiction. The production process and marketing opportunities differ for audiobooks, foreign translations, or multi-author collaborations. You also have to factor in qualifiers such as budget, skills, marketing goals, release frequency, and career level.

As such, we want to offer a list of common book release tasks—administrative, production, and marketing—and a basic timeline that you can customize to fit your business's needs. Use it as a starting point to develop a system that works for you and all your different releases, so you can skip the frantic, pulling-your-hair-out stage of publishing. Keep in mind these tasks and timelines are only suggestions. Your process and calendar will differ, so skip any steps that don't apply or tweak things as you go.

TIPS FOR CREATING A MANAGE-ABLE BOOK LAUNCH PROCESS AND CALENDAR

One of the biggest challenges in creating a book launch protocol is the array of strategies and techniques available to authors. Realistically evaluate your resources, especially time and money; your assets, such as established readership and number of published titles; and what you want to accomplish with your launch plan, which may include sales, series read-through, distribution to a new market, or establishing a name in a new subgenre or niche.

Tune in to the publishing community to learn what's working, learn about resources, and add new options. Beware, however, of FOMO, the fear of missing out. You do not—and should not—do what everyone else is doing. Some of the most successful authors focus inward to develop a highly personalized launch plan and tactics geared to their unique assets, readers, and priorities. Start small and build on your success, which means tracking each tactic and correlating results.

PRE-LAUNCH CONSIDERATIONS

Developing a book launch process and calendar is beneficial in that you don't need to "reinvent the wheel" every time you release a new book. A master checklist and timeline is a great starting place but may need adjustment. A few considerations:

Lead time: How soon before the release date can you finalize your manuscript? Is there sufficient time to solicit endorsements and professional reviews, which can require up to six months? If you use alpha or beta readers or an ARC team, have you factored this time into your production schedule?

Budget: Prioritizing outcomes is a good way to decide where to invest your marketing money. Researching costs and expenses is helpful for creating a realistic budget.

Soft or hard release: A soft release, where the book goes live before active marketing begins, might be a good option for new authors. It allows you to ensure all elements are accurate and in place. Authors may also choose to do a soft release to build organic momentum. Hard releases kick off with heavy marketing activities from the start.

PRE-LAUNCH SETUP

Before releasing a book, especially if you want to use marketing strategies, authors need to ensure the basic business structure is in place. This includes creating accounts at distributors or aggregators, building a website and/or landing page, developing a newsletter sign-up site, creating social media profiles, and setting up author profiles on Goodreads and BookBub.

PRE-LAUNCH PRODUCTION AND MARKETING

(2-6 months before launch)

Two to six months before a book's release, you're still solidly in the manuscript production stage of the publishing process. You've written "The End," but you're not done with the story just yet—over these next few weeks, you'll need to complete any last-minute editing and cleanup to the text and complete the layout for the formats you plan to publish. If you've got a planner, now is the time to put it to work; plug in your publish date, then spend some time backtracking to find the dates you'll need to send materials to your editor, street team, or cover designer.

- ☐ Complete manuscript
    - ☐ Gather feedback from alpha and/or beta readers
    - ☐ Self-edit manuscript
- ☐ Edit manuscript
    - ☐ Complete developmental edits
    - ☐ Complete line edits and/or proofread
    - ☐ Finalize manuscript
- ☐ Book cover production
    - ☐ Brainstorm cover art, fonts, color scheme, samples, and comparable titles
    - ☐ Commission book cover with designer
    - ☐ Obtain high-resolution covers for all assets (e-book, print, audio, etc.)
- ☐ Asset production
    - ☐ Identity formats and specifications for production (e-book, print, audiobook, ARCs, etc.)
    - ☐ Assemble materials needed for formatting: style guide, high-resolution cover(s), front and back matter, final edited manuscript, logos, chapter heading images, title page, etc.
    - ☐ Format book—outsource this or complete it yourself
    - ☐ Conduct quality check on all formatted assets
- ☐ Prepare front and back matter
    - ☐ Set up preorder for next book in series if including in back matter
- ☐ Write book description, tagline, short blurb, and full-length blurb
- ☐ Select excerpts, pull quotes, and teaser quotes
- ☐ Assemble assets (formatted files, covers, metadata) for upload to distributors
- ☐ Research and identify categories and keywords
- ☐ Set up preorder
- ☐ Assemble retailer links—created shortened links, if applicable
- ☐ Add book data and retailer links to website
- ☐ Book cover reveal blitz
- ☐ Recruit social media influencers and/or ARC team members

(2 months-2 weeks before launch)

Your story is polished; your cover is perfect. Now is the time to shout about it to your readers. From two months until about two weeks from launch day is the marketing stage, where you share the news about your new release with the world. Set up preorders, promote the book on social media and in your newsletter, and prepare any additional materials you want ready for once your book hits the shelves.

- ☐ Create graphics for social media, newsletter, blog, media kit, etc.
    - ☐ Preorder graphics
    - ☐ Cover reveal
    - ☐ Coming Soon
    - ☐ Now Available
    - ☐ Countdown
    - ☐ No text/evergreen version
- ☐ Add graphics to social media rotation
- ☐ Assemble media kit and/or sell sheet
- ☐ Preorder
    - ☐ Research preorder promotion available through retailers
    - ☐ Set up preorder giveaway
    - ☐ Announce in newsletter and on social media
- ☐ Cover reveal
    - ☐ Set up cover reveal giveaway
    - ☐ Announce cover reveal on social media and in newsletter
- ☐ Book paid promotions and advertisements—David Gaughran and Kindlepreneur offer helpful lists
- ☐ Request cross-promotion activities with peer authors
- ☐ Set up Goodreads giveaway
- ☐ Add book to BookBub profile, Amazon Author Page
- ☐ Create, format, and set up distribution for bonus content
- ☐ Prepare marketing and ad copy
- ☐ Distribute ARCs to readers, reviewers, and influencers
- ☐ Schedule release day celebration activities
    - ☐ Blog tour
    - ☐ New release takeovers
    - ☐ Cross-promotion events
- ☐ Design and order marketing collateral (bookmarks, postcards, etc.)
- ☐ Update back matter of previously published books

LAUNCH DAY PRODUCTION AND MARKETING

(1-2 weeks before launch)

It's release day! Today is a celebration of all the hard work you've put in these past few months—and that's not including all the time you spent writing the story before that. But your work still isn't quite done. Make sure you take some extra time around launch day to set your book up for success: post about it to your readers, throw a launch party, set up advertisements, and begin tracking your sales. And take a moment to soak it all in. After all, you did it! Your book is finally out in the world.

- ☐ Upload final files to retailers ten to fourteen days before release
- ☐ Share media kit/graphics with author cross-promotion partners
- ☐ Promote new release
    - ☐ Send new release newsletter
    - ☐ Add new release teasers to social media rotation
- ☐ Engage and interact with readers and reviewers on social media
- ☐ Schedule or launch Facebook, AMS, and/or BookBub ads
- ☐ Promote backlist or other books in series—consider submitting for a BookBub Featured Deal
- ☐ Host new release celebration
- ☐ Announce new release giveaway

POST-LAUNCH PRODUCTION AND MARKETING

(1 week after launch and ongoing)

An author's work is never done. Your book may be in readers' hands, but to truly set it up for success, be sure to check in on it monthly or quarterly to update your ads, refine your metadata, and promote the book along with the rest of your backlist. After that, stretch those fingers—it's on to the next book!

- ☐ Monitor and adjust ads
- ☐ Track sales and correlate to promotional initiatives
- ☐ Continue cross-promotion activities (newsletter swaps, posting in other reader groups)
- ☐ Follow-up with reviewers and cross-promo partners who have not yet engaged
- ☐ Update/refine keywords and categories
- ☐ Add editorial reviews to retailer product page
- ☐ Update media kit
- ☐ Send follow-up newsletter with thank-you message and what's next
- ☐ Continue to seek marketing opportunities (seasonal, discounts, cross-promo, etc.)

WANT TO READ MORE?

There is no shortage of resources to help authors develop a process that can be replicated and customized for each launch. Here are just a few:

- *My Book Launch Planner* (2023) by Mandi Lynn and Stone Ridge Books
- *How To Launch A Successful Series: Your Book Launch Survival Guide* (2023) by Helen B. Scheuerer
- *Successful Book Launch Secrets* (2020) by Donna Partow
- *Plan a Profitable Book Launch* (2021) by Mandi Lynn and Bethany Atazadeh
- *Release Strategies: Plan Your Self-Publishing Schedule for Maximum Benefit* (2019) by Craig Martelle and Michael Anderle
- *Launch That Book* (2023) by Tammy Karasek
- *The Nonfiction Book Publishing Plan* (2018) by Stephanie Chandler and Karl W. Palachuk
- *How to Revise and Re-Release Your Book* (2018) by Penny C. Sansevieri
- *Writing and Releasing Rapidly* (2019), *Writing and Marketing Systems* (2020), and Writing and Launching a Bestseller (2021) by Elana M Johnson
- *Romance Your Plan* (2020) by Zoe York ■

Maria Connor

Maria Connor

Maria Connor is the founder and owner of My Author Concierge, which provides high-level project management support services to self-published authors, She is the author of The Self-Publishing Checklist Series, a USA Today bestselling contemporary romance author, and an international speaker on writing, editing, marketing, and publishing topics. Since 2010, she has worked with more than a hundred authors across all genres, published more than 35 titles herself, and presented more than 30 workshops regionally, nationally, and internationally.

Exploring Kickstarter in 2024

A FRESH LOOK AT INNOVATIONS AND CROWDFUNDING STRATEGIES FOR AUTHORS

Kickstarter has long been a dynamic platform for creators to bring their projects to life, and 2024 is no exception. Kickstarter is a crowdfunding platform that empowers creators to turn their ideas into reality by engaging with a community of backers. Creators set a funding goal, select a timeframe for their campaign, and offer a range of rewards to backers based on their level of support, and supporters are only charged if the campaign funds fully.

While the fundamentals of Kickstarter remain a powerful force, recent trends have introduced new possibilities and strategies for authors looking to launch and fund their creative endeavors with the platform. We spoke to Kickstarter gurus Paddy Finn and Anthea Sharp about their 2024 Kickstarter tips and what authors need to know.

PADDY FINN

After finding success as a Science Fiction and Fantasy indie author, Paddy Finn saw another opportunity to build an audience and connect with his readers while funding his projects. Two years later, he'd raised seven figures on Kickstarter. Finn has just launched a Kickstarter masterclass where he shares everything he's learned about generating funding. Here are his insights and tips for 2024.

On Enhanced Backer Engagement Tools

BackerKit is management software that helps crowdfunded project creators raise additional funds, reach new backers, and solve their fulfillment logistics. It is a suite of tools or add-ons that can manage your pledges and give your backers more opportunities to contribute to your campaign by

- gathering and keeping backer info sorted with surveys,
- creating add-ons that give backers more opportunities to contribute,
- keeping momentum going with a preorder website,
- driving pledges from your community with BackerKit Launch, and
- reaching new backers using BackerKit Marketing.

"I see a lot of creators, including experienced creators, not using BackerKit's suite of tools to engage with their audience," Finn says. "That blows my mind. … BackerKit Launch is like email marketing on steroids. BackerKit Pledge Manager creates great cross-selling opportunities. And when you establish yourself in the market, BackerKit Marketing will consider running Facebook Ads campaigns on your behalf."

On Integrating Drop-Shipping with Your Campaign

"If you run a successful Kickstarter campaign that requires printing one thousand or more books, you might want to consider offset printing instead of print-on-demand," Finn says. "Instead of shipping all the product yourself, you can hook up with a fulfillment company who'll do it for you. In fact, if you work with the right people, they'll take care of everything from the boxes leaving the printer to the packages arriving in your backer's mail, allowing you to focus on writing without having to deal with packaging or admin. That said, I've seen some recent print-on-demand prices compete with smaller offset print runs of one thousand-plus units, so you might need to shop around or wait until you need a bigger lot."

A fulfillment partner can do all the legwork that goes into getting rewards and perks out on time. Some fulfillment companies worth checking out include Fulfillrite, Easy Ship, Floship, Shipwire, Shipbob, InterFulfillment, and Shipmonk.

On Early Bird Rewards

Early bird rewards are early incentives that encourage backers to support your campaign as soon as it launches. When using this strategy, project creators offer exclusive rewards or discounted prices for a limited number of backers who pledge their support early on, creating a sense of urgency for backers who want to secure these special rewards. It also helps establish a strong foundation of support, which can attract additional backers who are drawn to the momentum and excitement surrounding the campaign.

"Many backers on Kickstarter love collecting limited editions, and making a reward exclusive to your campaign is a great way to convert those people to pledges," Finn says. He recommends not posting early bird rewards as a separate reward tier for your campaign "because when people see that they missed that tier, it might turn them off. I would recommend instead offering an early bird reward in the body of your campaign. That way you can remove it when the early bird window has passed, and new backers who can't get it won't be upset."

On Backer Involvement in Decision-Making

Don't be afraid to reach out directly to those funding your campaign. "Backers are all too happy to tell you what they want. We've used backer polls to this effect," Finn says. "They've helped us figure out what backers would like us to create next and what they would be happy to pay for certain products."

Final Thoughts

"I like to tell creators new to Kickstarter to think big but start small. In other words, don't waste your big idea on your first Kickstarter, where you're still learning the ropes, because your big idea deserves better," he says. "Instead, run a small campaign related to that big idea. For example, if you want to fund a new series, run a smaller campaign for a prequel novella or short story collection first. That way you can learn without worrying, and you also build a small following that will boost the big campaign when you get to it."

ANTHEA SHARP

Anthea Sharp is a USA Today bestselling author, platform pro, and experienced creator who has successfully run seven book project campaigns on Kickstarter, funding nearly $70,000, plus helped scores of authors set up and launch their own. Sharp has published her lessons learned in her book *Kickstarter for Authors* and shares her tips for 2024 below.

On Connecting with Backers

"Kickstarter is a naturally interactive place, and many backers love the direct engagement they get to have with creators," Sharp says. "As well as using regular backer updates, authors are getting clever about finding ways to connect with supporters and get input on their projects while the campaign is in process. I've seen authors invite feedback via the comments section on the campaign itself, or via Google surveys or other poll options. … If you're the type of author who enjoys engaging with your readers, definitely lean into this aspect of running a campaign."

On Strategic Stretch Goals

"Early bird rewards are a time-honored way to give your campaign a strong launch while rewarding your first supporters who help get your project off the ground," Sharp says. "Some authors give a slight discount on one or more of their tiers, while others add extra perks or a bonus piece of swag to early backers. There's no one way to do it, and they're not required, but as more authors start using Kickstarter, it's one of many tools you can use to help make your campaign a success.

"Stretch goals, stretch rewards, and backer bonuses are also in the toolbox for keeping your campaign moving, rewarding your backers with extras, and helping sustain the excitement of a project beyond the first few days," she continues. "My most important piece of advice is to not put your monetary goals for unlocking your stretch goals," or goals that extend your campaign's funding goals after your initial benchmark is reached, "in the campaign details until after you've hit your funding goal. Especially if this is your first campaign, chances are very good you're guessed wrong in one direction or the other. It's always best to wait and see what your funding velocity looks like, and then decide where to set those goals."

On Social Media

"Definitely plan to post regularly on your social media about your Kickstarter campaign," Sharp says. "Use a number of different approaches: one day talk about the artwork, the next highlight the bonus goodies, the third do a deep dive about your characters, etc. Provide something interesting and different in each post. Also, if you're thinking of doing a Kickstarter campaign in the future, start supporting projects now, and post about them to your readers and fans. Warm up your newsletter audience. Make it clear that Kickstarter is a place where creative projects come to life, and supporters get to basically 'preorder' the books while directly supporting the author, plus get bonus goodies in the bargain." ∎

Tanya Nellestein

Tanya Nellestein

Tanya Nellestein is an avid reader, experience enthusiast, outstanding car vocalist, and Queen of fancy dress. In her spare time she is also a bestselling and award-winning author and journalist with a penchant for bloodthirsty battles and steamy romance. From Vikings to present day, Tanya writes page-turning, gut-churning stories with a romantic angle that always includes good sex and a happily ever after - eventually. Her debut novel, The Valkyrie's Viking recently hit Amazon's best seller list and her sixth novel, This Side of Fate, was the 2022 winner of the Romance Writers of Australia Sapphire Award for Best Unpublished Romance Manuscript. In 2021, Tanya won the Romance Writers of Australia Romance in Media Award. Tanya lives on the outskirts of Sydney, Australia amidst a cavalcade of never ending disasters, both natural and those of her own making.

From the Stacks

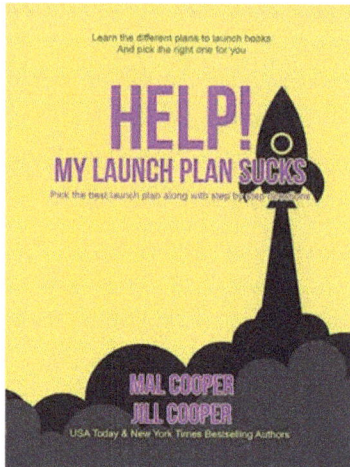

Help! My Launch Plan Sucks **by Mal and Jill Cooper**
https://books2read.com/u/4NwgEN

There's no singular right way to launch a book or series—at least, not one that will apply to everyone across the board. In their book, *Help! My Launch Plan Sucks*, Mal and Jill Cooper of The Writing Wives explore a range of options to answer your questions about each and help you find the method that will work best for your book. With definitions of common industry terms and worksheets to help you fill out your pre-publication calendar, the guide will walk you through every step of the process so that, by the end, you're ready to go for launch.

WideWizard
https://widewizard.co

Before you can celebrate your book's launch, you have to upload it to your distributors, and if you're publishing wide, that can be a daunting task. WideWizard can make it less so, saving you time and keeping you organized. The free auto-fill extension for Google Chrome or Firefox allows authors to input data like title, keywords, descriptions, and other metadata once; the extension will then copy that data into the appropriate fields on any compatible sites you visit, including Amazon, Draft-2Digital, Kobo, Booksprout, Google Play, or even Goodreads.

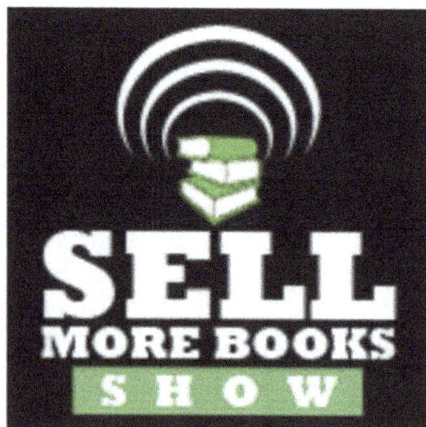

Sell More Books Show
https://www.sellmorebooksshow.com

With more than five hundred episodes to date, this weekly podcast, hosted by Bryan Cohen and H. Claire Taylor, offers listeners a deep dive into the most up-to-date news and sales strategies from the indie publishing industry. Each episode, Cohen and Taylor explore marketing methods that can appeal to every author, whether you're new or experienced, and frequently feature well-known guest speakers from across the community.

Nothing 'Lucky' about It

DOES YOUR STORY'S MAIN CHARACTER HAVE ENOUGH AGENCY?

In one episode of the TV sitcom *The Big Bang Theory*, several of the characters get disappointed after they realize the hero of *Raiders of the Lost Ark*, Indiana Jones, does nothing to affect the outcome of the story. Though they love the movie, that realization ruins the narrative.

This mirrors a common mistake authors make: the protagonist doesn't significantly affect the outcome of the story—in other words, the main character doesn't have enough agency. The main character reacts to everything around them rather than making things happen. "The reader is most invested in the protagonist above all other characters, so we want to see them do things in the story," writes developmental editor Alyssa Matesic in her craft blog.

In the Mystery genre, if sleuths don't have agency, they don't solve the murder. Instead, they often stumble upon the killer and conclude the case through happenstance. To the author, this can feel like the sleuth solves the murder—but that's not the case. In Romance novels, a romantic lead without agency reacts to everything happening around her without making deliberate choices that move the relationship forward. In Action-Adventure or Horror books, a hero without agency simply tries to survive and doesn't try to attain an overarching goal, making no choices that propel the plot.

As writing guide author K.M. Weiland notes in her blog, Helping Writers Become Authors, "a character with little to no agency won't be able to generate and/or respond to conflict"—which can drag the entire plot to a standstill. Thankfully, the problem is one you, as the author, have agency to fix.

GOALS AND MOTIVATIONS

This notion of agency—and the reader dissatisfaction that results—is rooted in two questions that go unanswered:

- What does my main character want?
- Why does my character want it? (What is their motivation?)

Main characters who primarily react have a difficult time pursuing their goals—and readers therefore can't easily identify those goals. If the main character's motivation is unclear, the plot is driftless—and readers don't know what to root for.

IDENTIFYING AGENCY ISSUES

If you're worried about your main character's agency, ask yourself these questions: does the climax of the scene, section, or book result from my main character's choices, or do external forces or other characters' actions lead the plot? Next, ask if the climax's resolution results from the main character's choices. If the answer to either question is "no," you have work to do.

The fix might be easier than you think. Many times, at crucial points in the plot, the author can add a choice for the protagonist that changes the plot from happenstance to increased agency. Often, a handful of scenes, several lines, or even a single paragraph will help fix the problem.

Let's say a Mystery has a climax where the amateur sleuth is in close quarters with the murderer. However, the sleuth doesn't realize the murderer's identity yet. The murderer attacks the sleuth; the sleuth then gets away, and the murderer is captured. This will often feel like happenstance and be unsatisfying for the reader.

To fix this problem, the author can make the following tweaks:

- The sleuth, throughout the book, uncovers a series of clues that reveal the killer's identity. This might require a new scene or a couple extra lines where the sleuth finds another clue.
- During the climax, when the sleuth is in close quarters with the killer, the sleuth discovers something—or may be triggered by a word, phrase, or object referenced earlier—that makes the puzzle lock into place.

Using something the sleuth learned previously in the book, the sleuth helps with the capture of the murderer.

Similar changes can be made for other genres. For Romance, the love interest revealing something emotional may allow the protagonist to later make a love connection. The climax can be the protagonist's "grand gesture" that references those earlier emotional reveals. In an Action-Adventure, add a few lines where the hero learns something that will be critical to how to defeat the evil forces.

These changes don't require wholesale rewriting, and they don't require reworking your protagonist's personality. With a few added scenes, a few added lines, and one or two one-line references spaced appropriately, you can often improve the main character's goals, motivations, and agency throughout your story, leaving the reader much more satisfied by the end. ■

Paul Austin Ardoin

Paul Austin Ardoin

Paul Austin Ardoin is the USA TODAY bestselling indie author of The Fenway Stevenson Mysteries and The Woodhead & Becker Mysteries. He holds a B.A. in creative writing from the University of California, Santa Barbara and an M.B.A. in marketing from the University of Phoenix. His book Zero to Four Figures: Making $1,000 a Month with Self-Published Fiction is scheduled for publication in June 2023.

PROSPERITY

A Money Mindset Reset

These days, everywhere you look, you'll hear book recommendations, podcast conversations, and articles like this one suggesting that working on your money mindset is the way to go.

And of course, I agree wholeheartedly. What you focus on expands. This includes your money mindset, which directly impacts your income—and yes, that includes your writing income.

What you might not know is exactly how to work on your money mindset, so allow me to go "inside baseball" on how I jumped from making five to six and even seven figures from my writing.

Step One: Dial up your personal conviction, and line your path with unstoppable self-confidence. You might currently be full of doubts, insecurities, and impostor syndrome (and if you don't have any of these, no need to order them from Amazon Prime). You must first believe you can earn a living as a writer—an abundant living, in fact—before it will happen. The fastest path to an unshakable money mindset is to define and reinforce it through a consistent daily ritual.

Step Two: Reinforce your mindset daily. Just as you must brush your teeth and take a shower daily, your mindset requires the same constant attention. Every morning, before I speak to another person, I talk to myself. I say, write, and read positive, present-tense affirmations using an app called ThinkUp and my journal. The app is great for recording all of those great things you need to tell yourself so that your subconscious mind can begin to work on your behalf. Writing the words is another way to lay those neural pathways.

3

Step Three: Speaking of your subconscious mind, do some daily reading to up-level your money mindset. I'm sure you've heard of GIGO (garbage in, garbage out). I changed it to mean "good stuff in, good stuff out." Reading just a few pages of positive content daily will reinforce that you can do it—whatever "it" is. *The Power of Your Subconscious Mind* by Joseph Murphy, *Psycho-Cybernetics* by Dr. Maxwell Maltz, and *The Power of Consistency* by Weldon Long are good places to start, as is *Think & Grow Rich* by Napoleon Hill if you want a money-focused title to add to the pile.

4

Step Four: Do the work. Once you have expanded your mindset, the money will follow—but only if you do the work. Reading, writing, and saying positive words won't necessarily mean money jumps right into your bank account. You'll be well served to identify the habits that coincide with the money mindset you've developed. But guess what, sparky? This is where the magic happens. Mindset plus habits equals making a living as a writer.

5

Step Five: Rinse and repeat. Many of the people in my life all say the same thing about me: I'm consistent. Whoopee! That doesn't blow my hair back, for sure, but it does allow a line of sight to how I get great results year in and year out. I do all of those steps, and I never miss a day. It's not sexy or exciting, but it is effective.

Allow me to end with this: you can get wherever you want to go; all you need to do is focus on your mindset. It really is that simple.

Happy writing! ■

Honorée Corder

Honorée Corder

Honorée Corder is the author of more than fifty books, an empire builder, and encourager of writers. When she's not writing, she's spoiling her dog and two cats, eating something fabulous her husband made on the grill, working out, or reading. She hopes this article made a positive impact on your life, and if it did, you'll reach out to her via HonoreeCorder.com.

Unleash Your Creative Juices: The Science Behind Brain.FM for Authors

Facing the blank page, with the cursor blinking like a beacon of wasted time, writers often find themselves in a silent standoff with their own creativity. The challenge goes beyond simply putting words on a page; it's about summoning the muse, maintaining focus, and breaking through the barriers of writer's block. This is where Brain.FM steps in with its own novel solution.

Brain.FM is a science-based music app that offers users different channels of background noise meant to make it easier to focus, relax, sleep, or meditate. Subscribed users select what they're hoping to achieve, then set timers in thirty-minute increments to listen for up to two hours or choose the infinity setting for uninterrupted listening. The premise of Brain.FM is not just to provide a background soundtrack for your writing sessions but also to enhance your cognitive functions, allowing for deeper focus, creativity, and productivity.

At the heart of Brain.FM's effectiveness is a technique known as active brain-state modulation. This method leverages a blend of musical compositions and soundscapes

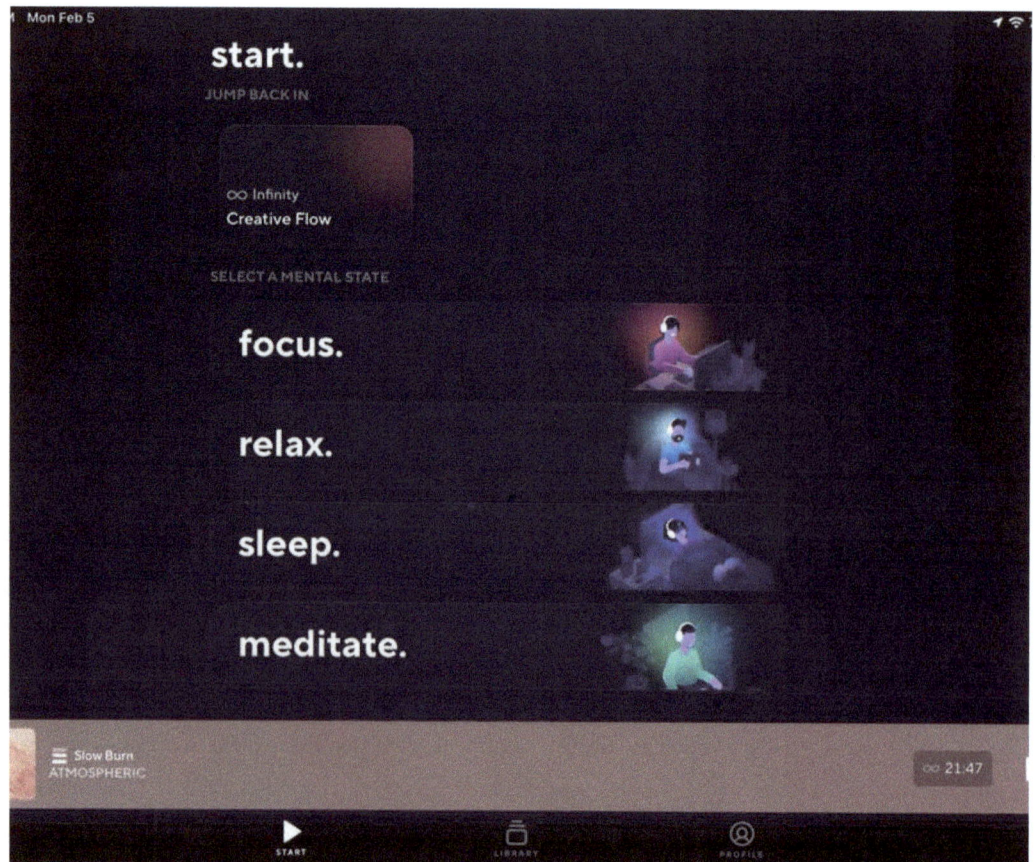

designed to influence the listener's brainwave patterns. Studies have shown that different brainwave patterns are associated with various states of consciousness. Alpha waves predominate during periods of relaxation, promoting a reflective and calm state of mind. But when a task demands attention and cognitive engagement, the brain generates beta waves, which are linked to alertness and focus.

Initially, the concept sounds similar to binaural beats, tones played at specific frequencies that are said to help your brain relax—but Brain.FM relies on a variety of different sound designs and techniques other than binaural beats, according to its website, and even offers a host of neuroscientific studies to support its claims. Scientific evidence for the benefits of binaural beats, by comparison, is limited.

Brain.FM is available on the iOS App or Google Play stores for mobile devices or via the website and costs $9.99 per month or $69.99 per year. As a productivity tool, it may seem to blend in with other apps available to authors that provide background music, block out distractions, and provide focus timers. But the added science behind this one may just make it worthy of your attention—as long as it's not when you're supposed to be writing.

Chelle Honiker

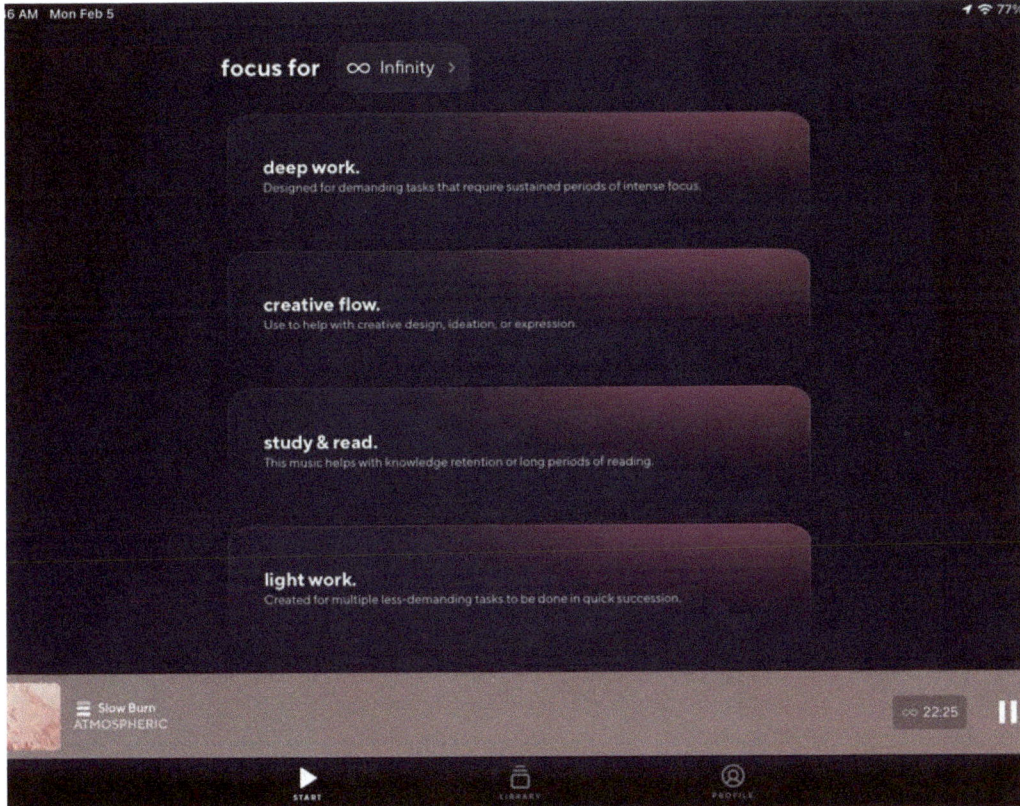

Chelle Honiker

Chelle Honiker is an advocate for the empowerment of authorpreneurs, recognizing the importance of authors taking charge of both their craft and careers. In response to this need, she has founded a media and training company dedicated to supporting these creative professionals. As the co-founder and publisher of Indie Author Magazine, IndieAuthorTraining, Indie Author Tools, and Direct2Readers.com, Chelle's team of more than 80 writers, editors, trainers, and support staff provides resources and insights that help authors navigate the complexities of self-publishing. Her role as the programming director for Author Nation, an annual conference in Las Vegas, further exemplifies her commitment to fostering a community where authors can grow and succeed. With a career spanning over two decades in executive operations and leadership, Chelle has honed her skills in managing complex projects and delivering impactful training programs. Her experience as a speaker and TEDx Organizer has taken her to many countries, where she has shared her insights with diverse audiences.

The Miniscule Tool that Can Transform Your Facebook Ad Campaigns

The Facebook pixel—recently renamed the Meta pixel—is a small piece of JavaScript code you can place on your website. The pixel gives you insights into how your audience interacts with your Facebook Ads. It also provides data on how Facebook users behave on your website after they click on an ad.

Now, that might read like a bunch of technical gobbledegook, but what it means is that you can use it to know more about what your ads are doing.

If you are yet to activate yours, it is a very simple process for which you can find a thousand YouTube tutorials. It will take less than an hour of your time to set it up.

But what do you do with it then, and how can you use it to make more money and sell more books?

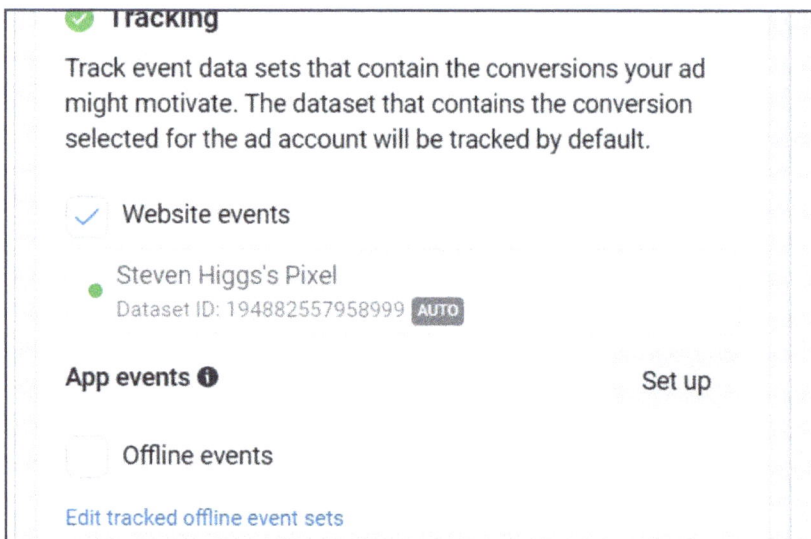

The pixel on one of my Facebook (Meta) Ads.

The pixel on your Facebook (Meta) Ads sits there quietly monitoring the activity being fed back to it. From where? Well, from your website is arguably the best place, but you can embed your pixel other places too.

For instance, if you have a funnel story on Bookfunnel that you give away for free, you can apply the pixel to it, and Facebook will identify the customers and log their information—not in a creepy anti-GDPR way, but benignly. You can use this information to build an audience; Facebook will build an avatar based on the overlapping characteristics of the people who went to Bookfunnel to get your free story, which you can use to target your advertising.

This task is performed in your ads manager under the Audience tab. Click to create a new audience, then select "Website."

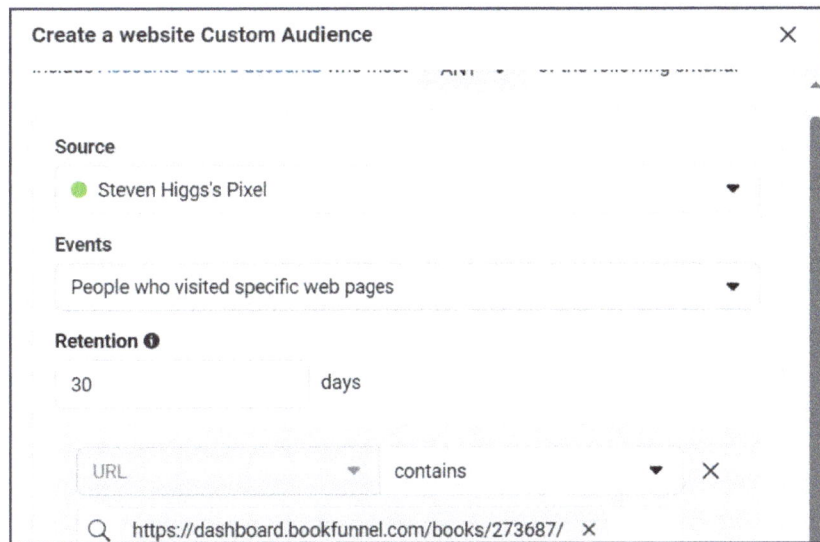

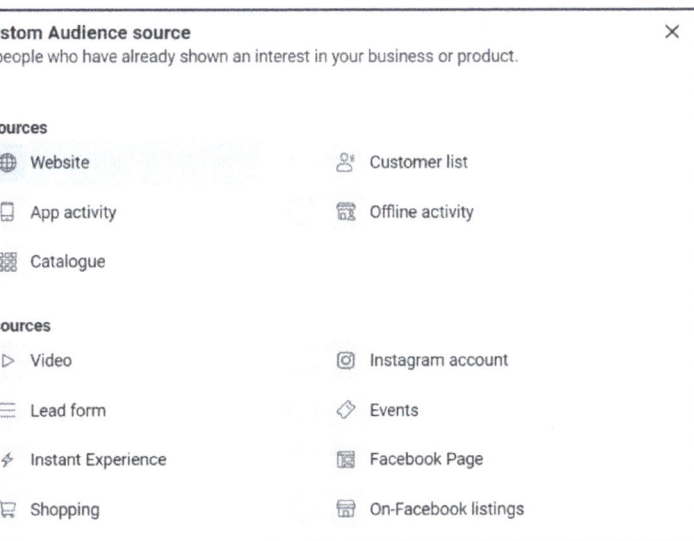

To create a custom avatar of people flagged by your Facebook pixel, visit your ads manager under the Audience tab, then select "Website."

This will take you to a new page. In Events, select "People who visited selected web pages," take the URL from the page for your free book, name the audience, and that's about it. The audience will take a few hours or maybe even a day to populate, but when it does, you will have an audience of millions of people Facebook has found that match exactly the characteristics of the people you attracted to your book—aka people who are likely to want to read your books.

To finish creating the target audience gathered from your Facebook pixel, select "People who visited selected web pages" in the Events tab, take the URL from the page for your free book, and give your group a name.

You can do much the same by writing a short story, putting it on a page at the back end of your website—not accessible from the homepage—and driving traffic to it from your newsletter, your social media, and through your books. It could even be a bonus chapter for your next release; it doesn't have to be a complete story.

Using the pixel in conjunction with the online store on your website, you can keep track of customer data, understand who is buying what, what the average customer spends, and what your bestselling products are. This enables you to tailor your efforts and get that customer to buy the boxed set and merch, not just the single title they came for.

This type of audience has often proved to be my most successful. The traffic you send, and that Facebook records, is made entirely of people who like your books enough to be following you already.

However—and this is a big however—if you are moving into direct sales, the Facebook pixel is everything. The subject is too big for just one article, but we'll explore it more in-depth in a future issue, and there are plenty of tutorials available for free via the internet.

Good luck! ■

Steve Higgs

Steve Higgs

High school Valedictorian enlists in the Marine Corps under a guaranteed tank contract. An inauspicious start that was quickly superseded by excelling in language study.

PLANNING TRAVEL TO A CONFERENCE?

Use miles.

Explore ways to make the most of your award miles.

Writelink.to/unitedair

YOUR ONE-STOP RESOURCE
INDIE AUTHOR TOOLS
INDIEAUTHORTOOLS.COM
📚 Over 45+ categories of resources, from AI to website builders, all designed to supercharge your self-publishing journey.
✍️ Authentic reviews and real-world case studies from authors who've used these tools to bring their creative visions to life.
👤 A community-powered project, crowdsourced by authors who know exactly what you need because they've been there too!
🚀 Boost your authorial prowess with our popular weekly newsletter, packed with tips, tricks, and updates on the latest tools.

www.ingramcontent.com/pod-product-compliance
Lightning Source LLC
Chambersburg PA
CBHW042341030426
42335CB00030B/3424